SPLIT INFINITIVE PRESENTS

A Caravan Named Desire

by Alexander Millington

Published by Playdead Press 2023

© Alexander Millington 2023

Alexander Millington has asserted his rights under the Copyright, Design and Patents Act, 1988, to be identified as the author of this work.

A CIP catalogue record for this book is available from the British Library.

ISBN 978-1-915533-15-9

Caution
All rights whatsoever in this play are strictly reserved and application for performance should be sought through the author before rehearsals begin. No performance may be given unless a license has been obtained.

This book is sold subject to the condition that it shall not by way of trade or otherwise, be lent, resold, hired out, or otherwise circulated without the publisher's prior consent in any form of binding or cover other than that in which it is published and without a similar condition including this condition being imposed on the subsequent purchaser.

Playdead Press
www.playdeadpress.com

CONTENTS

An introduction to *A Caravan Named Desire*   9

A Caravan Named Desire

    The Real Script   13

    The Krystal Script   63

    The Kastor Script   131

A Caravan Named Desire was first performed at The Rotunda Theatre: Squeak as part of the Brighton Fringe on 28 May 2023. The cast was as follows:

Alexander/Gary   Alexander Millington

Helen/Krystal   Helen Millington

Director   Helen Millington
Set Design & Build   Lewis Ranshaw

The production was supported using public funding by the National Lottery through Arts Council England.

This text went to press before the end of rehearsals and may differ from the play as performed.

CAST AND CREATIVES

Alexander Millington | Writer & Performer

Alexander is an award nominated writer and performer and Creative Director of Split Infinitive. Alexander's theatrical credits include *I Heart Michael Ball* (2022/23 Tour), *Three Way* (2021/22 Tour), *The Impossible Dream* (The Stockwell Playhouse's One Act Play Festival), *The Understudies* (2016 Tour) and *The Concept of Love* (2012 & 2016). Alexander has also had work broadcast on BBC Radio including *Over Time* (2020) and *A Real Christmas* (2020). Alexander is acknowledged in the True Acting Institutes *Best Ten Minute Plays of 2019* for his play, *Window Shopping*. He has also collaborated on works with the American Dramatist Guild and New Works Playhouse for online performances of his work *Cigarettes & Chairs* (2021) and *For Better or For Worse* (2020).

Alexander is a Lecturer in Performing Arts, specialising in script writing, contemporary British theatre and solo performance. He is a Licentiate of Trinity College London and holds an MA in Playwriting from the University of Lincoln.

Helen Millington | Director & Performer

Helen is an award nominated director and Artistic Director of Split Infinitive. Helen has been directing, performing and producing theatre for 25 years and, as such, has gained extensive experience in a wide variety of performance related fields. She has previously performed with the Lincoln Shakespeare Company, in The Lincoln Mystery Plays, as Titania in a national tour of *A Midsummer Night's Dream* and has directed various productions including devised performances and children's theatre. Alongside Split Infinitive, Helen runs Lincoln School of Speech and Drama, is Secretary of The Lincoln Music & Drama Festival, spent several years as Head of Speech and Drama at Stamford Endowed Schools, and has adjudicated many poetry competitions. She is a member of the Society of Teachers of Speech and Drama and holds an MA in Contemporary British Theatre from the School of Fine and Performing Arts at the University of Lincoln. Through Split Infinitive, Helen has also previously worked on R&D sessions for projects including *Three Way* (2021), *I am an actor...* (2020), *Over Time* (2020) *Jump, Jump, Push* (2019), *New Year, Same Me* (2019), and *Child's Play* (2018).

SPLIT INFINITIVE

Split Infinitive is an award nominated, Lincolnshire based theatre company dedicated to creating intimate and engaging pieces of original theatre, which explore the dynamic between spectator and performer and examine the relationships created throughout our lives. Established in 2019, Split Infinitive has worked with local and emerging artists whilst developing new work. Since 2019, they have toured the UK performing in Brighton, London, Birmingham, Manchester, Oxford, Leicester and Bedford. They have been Off West-End Award nominated for their 2022 production of *I Heart Michael Ball* and have been praised by critics for creating performances heralded as 'experiential'. Alongside their theatre work, they have had performances broadcast on BBC Radio (*A Real Christmas* and *Over Time*) and, during the COVID pandemic, collaborated with other theatre companies in creating online performances.

Twitter	@SplitTheatre
Facebook	@SplitInfinitiveTheatre
Instagram	@SplitInfinitiveTheatre
Web	www.splitinfinitivetheatre.co.uk

ACKNOWLEDGEMENTS

Special thanks go to;

Lewis Ranshaw for his amazing photography throughout the rehearsal process and his engineering expertise and vision when deconstructing and reconstructing our caravan.

Graham Lowes for his continued support of our productions and for always being an ear when we constantly discuss our ideas with him.

And to all the people who kindly donated to our funding page and attended our scripted performances whilst we developed the script: Mary-Jane Ives, Oliver Marshall, Lynne Swift, Cathy Ashwin, Jonathan Whiting, Angela Wood, Karen Barrett, Sarah Baishaw, Andy Jordan, Tim Lee, Alissa Clarke, Elinor Parsons and to everyone else who has supported this endeavour.

An Introduction to
A Caravan Named Desire

As a theatre company that creates original pieces of theatre, exploring audience interaction and participation, playing with the relationship between audience and performer, we are regularly fascinated by the work of other artists, theatre makers and companies that are doing the same. We are inspired by the work of companies like Action Hero, YESYESNONO and Third Angel, and playwrights such as Tim Crouch who like to blur the lines between fact and fiction, play and reality, the stage and the auditorium. *A Caravan Named Desire*, similarly to our previous two productions, does all of these things, but why have we put three versions of it together in this book?

We wanted to create a collection that documented our progress through the rehearsal process and, more so than our previous productions, this has taken quite a bit of redrafting to get to where it is now (or, at least, as it is at time of publication – it may still change once we're on the road!). There are many reason why a script might go through redrafts and editing; creative choices, practicality, logistical issues, personnel issues, cast concerns, to name but a few. This introduction will briefly outline why and when changes occurred through the creative process which has led us to this publication.

As creatives and theatre makers who go through the redrafting process, we are always curious as to how many drafts top playwrights like Simon Stephens or Laura Wade get to before publication or opening night. Well, to put the record straight for us, for *A Caravan Named Desire*, this publication contains drafts 10 ('The Real Script'), 3 ('The Krystal Script') and 7 ('The Kastor Script'), though that's not to say we won't be on draft 11 by the time we reach our first show at Brighton.

A brief note on our process in general; different writers and theatre makers have different starting points for a new script/production: an image, a sentence, a character, etc. We start with a title! Hey, it works for us! *A Caravan Named Desire* was the title we decided upon for our third production and so that's what we worked with. The title gave us the initial idea of a sex worker and client relationship set within a caravan environment and from late night / early morning conversations, an idea had formed and the script writing began.

Our very first draft followed much the same form as 'The Krystal Script', included in this collection. A female sex worker, living in a caravan, who's just started seeing a new client who is having some sexual difficulties, and feels that seeing someone like Krystal will help him. This initial draft had our client in a generally monogamous homosexual relationship, however, after recently getting engaged, he wishes to explore his sexuality (with his partners permission) to try and discover his true desires. Although generally happy with this draft, following some read-throughs and workshops, we felt we were covering old ground, exploring male bisexuality in very similar ways as we had with our first production, *Three Way*. It was this draft which was originally performed at the LCB Depot in Leicester. 'The Krystal Draft' featured in this publication follows very much the ideas we used in draft one, but rather than it being an exploration of the clients own sexuality and desire, it was more a case of him trying to overcome his own sexual insecurities.

Due to unforeseen circumstances, however, we were required to recast roles, with the characters now being played by both members of Split Infinitive (Alexander and Helen). Due to our own comfort levels and wanting to play to our strengths as performers, the decision was quickly made to gender swap the two roles, making the male character the sex worker and the female character the client ('The Kastor Script').

Swapping the gender roles of the script initially seemed like a logical and seemingly easy task, however this led to some unexpected complications. Simply swapping the lines from female to male raised some fresh concerns. A line which was spoken by Krystal presented as strong, confident and feisty. However, when spoken by her male counterpart, Kastor, became predatory and overly aggressive. And lines from client, Gary, being shy, nervous and a little eccentric, when delivered by female client, Gabi, seemed unnecessarily meek and stereotypically two dimensional as a female character.

As 'The Kastor Script' developed through workshopping and rehearsals, something was still missing, the characters weren't connecting as they had in their previous incarnations. Were we reading into it too much? Were we too close to it? Had we fallen out of love with the idea? Or, is there really something to be said about how the characters' chemistry, even on the page, needs to 'pop'? There was only one thing left to do.

Talking through what originally brought us to the idea of the story, what excited us, and what made us excited about our previous work, we realised what it was missing – it was missing us!

Taking it back to its bones, to the character's we loved and whom we found interesting, Krystal and Gary, and by bringing ourselves into the story, *literally,* we fell in love with the narrative again. This is what brought us to The Real Draft. The draft that shows the development of a relationship. Of a partnership in flux. It just wasn't quite the relationship story we thought we'd be telling.

Helen and Alexander

A CARAVAN NAMED DESIRE
(THE REAL SCRIPT)

CHARACTERS

ALEXANDER
Early to mid 30s, a little past his best.

HELEN
Older than Alex, still in her prime.

This text went to press before the end of rehearsals and may differ from the play as performed.

Lines written in **bold** *are directly addressed to the audience. Wherever possible, the audience should be invited to join the conversations between Alexander and Helen.*

The stage is filled with an old caravan with one side removed so that the audience can see the action within. It has been cared for over the years, but some wear and tear is unavoidable. It looks like it hasn't been moved for a long time. When scenes are exterior to the caravan, they can be performed either in front of the removed wall or the caravan can be rotated. Outside the caravan there are some old camping chairs and a table. Unless otherwise stated, all scenes are at night and the lighting should demonstrate this. The interior of the caravan is lit with old lamps, fairy lights, and one single, bare hanging bulb in the centre of the main living space. The interior of the caravan is surprisingly clean and tidy, though very dated, possibly 80s or early 90s decor. It is cramped, and most of the furniture needs some form of unfolding or setting up.

Alexander and Helen are standing outside the caravan. They are looking at each other, both feel a mix of emotions; panic, excitement, nervousness, and fear. They stand in silence for a bit longer than a moment, just staring at each other.

HELEN Are you ready?

The lights blow and they are left in darkness.

Transition.

ALEXANDER Good evening everyone.

HELEN Good evening. I know what you're thinking. Shit! Where's the fucking fourth wall. These bastards could have me doing some kind of interactive shit.

ALEXANDER And maybe we will.

HELEN But not much.

ALEXANDER You see, that's the point of this really. Trust. You see, most of time you trust the performer not to talk to.

HELEN Touch you. I'm Helen by the way.

ALEXANDER And I'm Alexander. And this is our set.

HELEN It's a caravan.

ALEXANDER Well, it's a set made up to look like a caravan. This is where we need you to trust us, trust the set. Forget that we're currently in the [name of space] and believe we're actually outside, and occasionally inside, a caravan.

HELEN **Welcome to our new play...**

ALEXANDER *A Caravan Named Desire.*

HELEN I was going to say that.

ALEXANDER Sorry.

HELEN *A Caravan Named Desire.*

ALEXANDER **Better? Now, a little bit of back story before we start...**

HELEN Do we need it?

ALEXANDER What?

HELEN Do they need the back story? Why can't we just start?

ALEXANDER Because I think it's important for them to know why I wrote it.

HELEN **And I directed it by the way.**

ALEXANDER I knew you'd have to get that in.

HELEN Fine, just do your stupid intro so we can get started.

ALEXANDER Thank you. As I was saying, a bit of back story for why we've created this piece. I'm interested in sex. All aspects of it. Not in a pervy way, just a general... fascination. Why we do it, how we do it, who we do it with, and how we tell stories about it. And that's sort of what this play is, a story about sex. Sort of. You see I had this idea of writing a play which showed sex in all it's different guises: romantic, messy, boring, violent, exciting, mundane, angry, supportive, funny, embarrassing, regretful, memorable, forgettable, tender, heated, force of habit, ritualistic, just lubing up and getting on with it, the long build up with short lasting event, the spur of the moment that leads to an all-nighter, the...

HELEN Sixty minutes.

ALEXANDER But I knew I wouldn't be able to do this in just sixty minutes, so instead I thought about telling the story of a prostitute – or sex worker as they are now known - and a client and how their relationship potentially led to a variety of different sex acts.

HELEN But that idea was also dull.

ALEXANDER It was fine.

HELEN	So he thought why not tell a true story of a sex worker and client relationship. But it turns out not many clients want to make friends with their sex provider, or vice versa, and not many want their story to be told.
ALEXANDER	So I had no choice.
HELEN	No choice?
ALEXANDER	No. I had no choice but to investigate the matter myself. So I began to see a sex worker. Write what you know, they always say, so I had to make sure I knew. Now, a lot of what you are going to see tonight is true, by which I mean a representation of the truth, of events that have happened. A dramatisation of real life, real events. Inspired by, based upon. Not exactly a fallacy, more of an interpretation. What I'm trying to say is that this is all true, completely true... except for the bits that aren't.
HELEN	Now, before we go any further, do we have any questions? Have we said anything that has been unclear at all?
ALEXANDER	Good. One last formality then. I know I've already introduced myself to you as Alexander, but for the majority of this

performance I will be referred to as Gary – the reasons for which will become clear to you.

So, yes, I will be playing the part of Gary, and my wife, Helen, will be playing the part of our sex worker...

HELEN   Krystal

ALEXANDER   Yes. Now, do you want to get yourself ready?

HELEN   Ready?

ALEXANDER   Costume.

HELEN   What costume?

Alexander grabs a leopard print top and scarf from inside the caravan.

ALEXANDER   This.

HELEN   I'm not wearing that! I'll look like Bet Lynch!

ALEXANDER   That's a dated reference.

HELEN   We said we would be avoiding stereotypes.

ALEXANDER   So what, you're just going to wear that?

HELEN   Yes!

ALEXANDER   But...

HELEN   Who's the director.

Alexander sulks for a moment.

                    I'll wear the animal print scarf if you insist but that's it.

ALEXANDER   I've put your shoes in the caravan too.

He gestures to a pair of heels.

HELEN   I'm not wearing those either. I can't walk in heels and you know that.

ALEXANDER   So what then? Slippers?

HELEN   I'm at home, I'm comfortable, yes!

ALEXANDER   Fine.

HELEN   Shall I go now?

ALEXANDER   You're the director.

Helen positions herself in the caravan.

ALEXANDER   **Now… erm… well, I think we can get started now.**

Transition.

Krystal climbs back into the caravan and begins hunting for a light bulb. Once she has found one she replaces the bulb that blew, and the lights come back on completely red. There is a knocking at the door.

KRYSTAL   Just a minute!

Krystal then turns on a lamp with a clear bulb to balance the light. Gary is waiting at the caravan door wearing a cheap-looking button-through shirt and trousers, as if he has just come from work. Everything is a little bit creased, and clearly a little bit old. He knocks again.

>Just a sec!

Krystal turns on some fairy lights that trail around the caravan. She has to click the button a few times to work through the pre-sets before she settles on one. She checks herself in a small mirror before going to the door and opening it.

> Sorry about that, bloody fuse went again. It's always doing it. Are you the new guy Uncle Stanley was on about? I'll just be a sec, come in.

Gary enters and is directed across to the other end of the caravan. Krystal goes to the bathroom, the only place not entirely visible to Gary, but is to the audience. Krystal pulls out a small money bag from within the toilet cistern. It contains some notes. She pulls out a few notes and returns the remaining money to where she found it. She returns to Gary.

> I told Stanley it was going to be a bit short this month 'cause the internet kept cutting out, so my loss of income is due to him. He knows, he said it's fine so no need to bother him. Well here, aren't you going to take it?

Krystal thrusts the money towards Gary. Gary, uncertain of what to do, slowly reaches for the money. Before he touches it, Krystal pulls it back.

	Hang on. What's your name again?
GARY	Gary. My name's Gary.
KRYSTAL	You're not the guy Uncle Stanley was on about.
GARY	Erm… no. I don't know any Stanley. I sent you a message last week. We'd arranged to meet.
KRYSTAL	Thursday. We said we'd meet on Thursday. It's not fucking Thursday today is it?
GARY	No. No, it's Wednesday today.
KRYSTAL	We did say Thursday, didn't we?
GARY	Oh yes, we did. I'm early.
KRYSTAL	By twenty-four-fucking-hours. You made me think I'd lost a fucking day or something, Jesus Christ! You don't do that to somebody! Do you have any idea what shit you might have caused by making me think I'd lost a day. I might have plans, very specific plans, you know, which I have to do on a Thursday and now all of a sudden I've lost my Thursday and forgotten to do everything!

GARY It's not Thursday though, it's Wednesday.

KRYSTAL I know that now! I knew that five minutes ago. But the time between five minutes ago and now I thought it was fucking Thursday! Fuck me I need a sit down.

GARY I'm sorry.

Krystal tucks the cash into her clothes.

KRYSTAL I should think so too. Why are you here anyway?

GARY I just, I wanted to make sure I knew the way when I came tomorrow, you know. Make sure I didn't get lost. Or that it wasn't some fake address or something. So, I put the address you gave me into my phone and, as you said, it directed me to this site, and then I saw the caravan and thought, well, whilst I'm here I should probably just knock and check it's the right one. I didn't want to come tomorrow and find I was at the wrong door.

KRYSTAL Right, well… you've found me. Congratulations.

GARY Thank you.

Beat.

KRYSTAL Did you want anything else?

GARY   Oh, sorry, no. I just wanted to make sure I knew the way. I should be going actually. Nice to have met you.

KRYSTAL   Wait, wait, wait. Since you're here, do you want to…?

GARY   Oh, no, no thank you. I've got to get back. But I'll definitely be back tomorrow. I'll see myself out.

Gary goes to exit the caravan and closes the door behind him.

KRYSTAL   Alright. Well, see ya.

Transition.

ALEXANDER   I did actually turn up twenty-four hours early. She probably thought I was a proper weirdo. You see I really wanted you to see this as part of the story, how a seemingly bad impression can still lead to a lasting relationship. It's all part of the build-up you see, the lead in, the details that create that little je ne sais quoi.

HELEN   Would you just get ready for the next scene and stop monologuing. No one cares.

Alexander does as he is told by his director.

Transition.

Krystal is laid on the sofa bed going through some paperwork. She keeps looking at the clock hanging on the wall. She then taps on her phone to check the time is correct. Gary is outside the caravan, sitting in one of the camping chairs. Eventually, Krystal goes to the caravan door and opens it. She looks about until she spots Gary sitting in the chair and is startled.

KRYSTAL   Creeping Jesus! What the fuck are you doing sitting there?!

Gary is startled by her response.

GARY   Sorry. I came to your door, but I was a little early and wasn't sure if you might be busy, so I thought I'd just wait out here for a minute. I guess I must have lost track of time.

KRYSTAL   You were meant to have been here at seven.

GARY   I know.

KRYSTAL   It's nine!

GARY   I know. I lost track of time.

KRYSTAL   Fuck me.

GARY   Should I come back another time?

KRYSTAL   No. No, it's fine. I'm charging you as if you were here from seven though.

GARY   Ok.

KRYSTAL   (*to herself.*) Two fucking hours.

GARY   What do we do now then?

KRYSTAL   Do you wanna come in?

GARY   Can do.

KRYSTAL   Unless you wanna do it out here?

GARY   Would you like to?

KRYSTAL   I was kidding. It's fucking freezing out here.

GARY   Sorry.

Beat.

               It's a lovely night.

KRYSTAL   Yeah?

Krystal looks up at the sky.

               Yeah, I suppose it is.

GARY   The moon's so bright.

KRYSTAL   I prefer new moons myself.

GARY   Yeah?

KRYSTAL   You can see the stars better then. The moonlight blocks out a lot of the stars.

GARY   At New Moon you're also meant to bow and turn over any of your silver for good luck...

or a new love. My Aunty Blanche told me that.

KRYSTAL　　Yeah?

Beat

Well, come in then. I'm letting all the cold in here!

Gary gets up out of the chair and enters the caravan. Krystal shuts the door behind them.

I can see you're going to be trouble.

GARY　　I don't mean to be.

KRYSTAL　　I'm sure. You just go from twenty-four hours early to two hours late. What would you have done if someone else turned up?

GARY　　Erm... I don't really know. Left, I suppose.

KRYSTAL　　Well, you're lucky I'm quiet at the moment. And in a good mood. Look, why don't you take a seat. Do you want a drink?

GARY　　Oh, nothing for me, thank you.

KRYSTAL　　Then take a seat while I make myself a drink.

Krystal gets a bottle of squash and water out of a cupboard along with a glass and pours herself a drink. She takes a swig then tops up her glass. Gary is looking for somewhere to sit down. He goes to sit on the sofa bed but doesn't want to disturb the papers that are there. He starts to move some of them when Krystal turns around and sees him.

> Don't fucking look at those!

Krystal rushes across the caravan and grabs at the papers, piling them up and throwing them in a drawer.

GARY   I'm sorry. I was just trying to find somewhere to sit.

KRYSTAL   So you start looking over my fucking tax returns?

GARY   Tax returns?

Krystal takes Gary by the shoulders and places him on the sofa bed where she has created him a space.

KRYSTAL   Yeah, my fucking tax return. I'm not exactly PAYE doing this, am I? Now, just sit there, and don't move, alright.

GARY   Sorry.

KRYSTAL   And stop apologising.

Gary goes to apologise again but stops himself.

> Now, before we go any further, have you got money?

Gary reaches into his pocket and pulls out his wallet.

GARY	Did it not come through? I used the link you sent me when I booked.
KRYSTAL	That was for one hour. As I said, I'm charging you for three now.
GARY	Oh, yes. Sorry. How much? I've only got…
KRYSTAL	Hang on, let me work it out. Now, you've wasted two hours already, so that's going to be £160. £80 an hour whether we do anything or not, no negotiation. Now, what is it you actually want? You didn't go into much detail before.
GARY	Well…
KRYSTAL	As I said, I'm open to most things but I do have my limits.
GARY	All I really want is…
KRYSTAL	Come on, spit it out.
GARY	Can we just talk?
KRYSTAL	Talk?
GARY	Yeah.
KRYSTAL	I take it back, I will take the money first.
GARY	I'm not saying I definitely don't want to do anything, I'm just not sure that I will.

KRYSTAL   So what *might* you want to do? Hand jobs, blow jobs, just wanna fuck, if so, front or back? Wanna finger me? Go down on me? Give me a facial, fisting, pegging, rimming, be rimmed…?

GARY   I don't know. I probably won't want to try anything. At least not tonight. Maybe if we hit it off we could arrange a second night. I don't really know. I've never done this before. I'm sorry. Maybe I should just go now.

Gary gets up to leave but Krystal stands in his way.

KRYSTAL   £240 and you just wanna talk? Stay for the hour, and we'll talk. That's all that's covered, mind. Anything else happens and I charge more.

GARY   Ok.

Gary gets out his wallet again and takes out some money.

                 I've only got £50 with me.

KRYSTAL   I take card.

Gary takes out his phone to pay. Krystal picks up her card machine from amongst the paperwork on the bed. She sets it up using her phone. There's an awkward silence while Krystal waits for the machine to load. She offers the device to Gary.

                 Tap it.

Gary does so. The transaction goes through.

    Right. So, what do you wanna talk about?

Transition.

ALEXANDER **I hope this isn't breaking up the action too much for you. I don't mean it to, it's just there isn't much point in you watching the next hour when it's just talking. There wasn't even much of that actually, to be fair. There were probably more pauses and silences than talking. And there's no point me making you watch an hour of just pauses and silences. I mean you might as well go and watch a Beckett or a Pinter if you're just gonna watch a silent stage.**

    Anyway, you didn't miss much. I didn't really think much about the details when I booked the appointment so I didn't even think about whether I would tell the truth or not when I met her. I decided to tell her that I worked at the local council office. That I lived alone in a two up, two down house I rent from my mother.

Helen moves position to confront Alexander.

HELEN Hang on, I didn't know this. Why didn't you tell her the truth?

ALEXANDER   Because, I thought if I told her I was a writer trying to get a good story to make a play then she might not be as forthcoming.

HELEN   You could have still said you were married though. Married men still see sex workers don't they? In fact I imagine most people who see sex workers are married. So, why *did* you say you were seeing her?

ALEXANDER   I said I was a virgin and that I wanted to try it with a professional before I did it with anyone else.

HELEN   You'd rather tell people you're a thirty year old virgin than say you're married to me?

ALEXANDER   There's nothing wrong with being a thirty year old virgin. I just thought it might complicate things. Now, can we return to the story.

Helen reluctantly moves back into position.

ALEXANDER   As I was saying, we didn't do much on that first visit. We didn't actually do much for the first three visits. It was on my fourth visit however when I finally got up the nerve to… well, try something.

Transition.

Gary is pacing around outside the caravan. Krystal is standing at the door as before trying to convince him to come in.

KRYSTAL   Look, the longer you stay out here the colder my caravan's going to get and then we'll both be complaining. Now, why don't you just get in here and tell me what's shit in your knickers today?

GARY   Nothing's shit in my knickers!

             Do you like me?

KRYSTAL   Do I what?

GARY   Do you like me?

KRYSTAL   To be honest you're freaking me out a little bit.

GARY   I know you don't *like me* like me, that's not what I'm asking. What I'm asking is do you... do you think I'm an alright person.

KRYSTAL   I've only met you a handful of times and even then you barely speak, so I can't really say. I doubt you're a complete wanker if that's what you mean?

GARY   Ok.

KRYSTAL   I'm not saying I've completely ruled it out, mind.

GARY   I think I like you.

KRYSTAL   Right.

GARY   Not, like that. I could never like you like that.

KRYSTAL   Good to know.

GARY   I don't mean it like that. I just mean, I like you as a person, an acquaintance, sort of.

Beat.

             I don't think you're a complete wanker either.

They both smile. This is the first time they both seem relaxed.

KRYSTAL   Look, why don't you come in, I'll make us both a drink and we can have a chat again.

Krystal turns to get some cans of drink out of her cupboard. Gary just stands and stares at her.

GARY   I want to do more than just talk tonight.

Krystal turns to look at him.

             If that's ok.

KRYSTAL   Erm. Sure. Yeah. What did you have in mind?

GARY   I don't know.

KRYSTAL   Right.

GARY   I just… I want to try something new.

Pause.

KRYSTAL   Alright. I'll get those drinks.

Krystal gets out some cups to pour the drinks into but changes her mind.

GARY   I don't drink.

KRYSTAL   I get the impression you're going to need something. It's only coke anyway.

GARY   Can I just have a water?

KRYSTAL   Alright.

Krystal gets out a bottle of water and passes it to Gary. Gary just watches her, not thinking to take the bottle from her. Krystal just places it on the side. He takes a step towards her as if about to do something but is unsure what. He takes a step back, sees the water and takes a mouthful.

GARY   Do you kiss?

KRYSTAL   Kiss?

GARY   I know some…

KRYSTAL   Some?

GARY   What do you like to be called?

KRYSTAL   Krystal.

GARY   I mean…

KRYSTAL   I know what you mean. I'm Krystal.

GARY   Well, I just know some… Krystals that don't do kissing.

KRYSTAL   Know many Krystals do you?

GARY   Well, no. I mean I've heard, or rather seen on TV, that some don't like to do all that stuff.

KRYSTAL   Do you like to kiss?

Gary doesn't know how to respond for a second before eventually nodding.

              Then we can kiss.

GARY   Ok. Ok.

Krystal moves close to Gary. Gary stands still but begins to prepare himself for a kiss.

Transition.

ALEXANDER   **Her hands were all over me. Her fingers running through my hair, pulling my face into hers. I felt her fingers slowly run down my back before grabbing my arse. Our bodies rubbing together, her tits pressed up against me. I could feel her hands making their way round to my belt! She whipped it off me, ripped open her top and dropped to her knees…! I**

wish. Can you seriously imagine me...? We just kissed. But, you know what, she was pretty good. I was a little awkward at first as I warmed up into it but when we properly got going, I think I did a pretty good job too! It was a bit like being back in school. When you'd spend ages kissing and feel like you'd done so much together.

Who here remembers the name of their first kiss by the way, you don't need to call it out, just a show of hands. Everyone remembers their first. Ok, a little trickier now. Who remembers *how many* people they've kissed, the actual number, not a round abouts? And their names? So, we're not really all that different are we. Some of us, anyway. Selena was my first. Selena French.

HELEN	Can we stop indulging about your past flings and get going.

Transition.

KRYSTAL	So be honest, was that your first kiss?

Gary seems to be just staring off into the middle distance, holding his bottle of water.

GARY	No!
KRYSTAL	No?

GARY	Year 5. Selena French, at St Mary's Primary School. Kiss chase in the courtyard. I didn't even know I was playing but she just ran up to me, grabbed me, I mean properly grabbed me, and just planted one on my lips then ran off.
KRYSTAL	Did she kiss you as her name suggests?
GARY	Pardon?
KRYSTAL	French?
GARY	We were only nine.

Beat.

	I lied to you Krystal. I've been seeing someone.
KRYSTAL	Ok.
GARY	I'm not anymore!
KRYSTAL	Right.
GARY	But it was pretty serious.
KRYSTAL	Ok.
GARY	I just thought you should know.
KRYSTAL	Hang on, does this mean you're not a virgin?
GARY	Well, not exactly.

KRYSTAL   Well you either are or you're not. Either way, it doesn't really bother me. You can say what you want, you're paying for the time.

GARY   It's just, I'm a virgin in terms of… I've never really fully been with a woman.

KRYSTAL   What do you mean?

GARY   I'm… well, I struggle.

KRYSTAL   Right.

Transition.

ALEXANDER   I won't bore you with this next bit. It goes on a for a bit and it's not true anyway, so it doesn't really matter.

HELEN   Wait a minute, so you admit to her that you lied.

ALEXANDER   Yes.

HELEN   But rather than actually tell the truth, you just told another lie.

ALEXANDER   A more feasible one.

HELEN   And so now you're still not admitting you're married, but instead that you now can't get it up.

ALEXANDER   I can't keep it up.

HELEN   So erectile disfunction is still more preferable to a wife.

ALEXANDER   You know that's not what I'm saying.

HELEN   Just get on with it!

Transition.

KRYSTAL   But you do at least stay hard when you wank, right? You do wank don't you? Masturbate? Jerk off? Shake hands with the milkman? Polishing the banister? Celebrating Palm Sunday? Burping the worm? Making soup?

GARY   Erm… Do you mind if I just take a minute? I'm just getting a bit… sorry.

Gary rushes outside of the caravan to try and catch his breath. Krystal stands at the door of the caravan and watches him.

KRYSTAL   You alright?

GARY   No. I get like this. I don't really know why I'm here. I don't know what's wrong with me.

KRYSTAL   It's alright, just take a breath. Nothing's wrong with you. You want another water or something?

GARY   No, I'll be alright. I just need…

Gary sits down on one of the camping chairs again. He looks up at the sky.

                        You're right. You can see more stars without
                        the moon.

Krystal steps out of the caravan and looks up.

KRYSTAL   Beautiful, isn't it? If you look over there
                you'll see the Big Dipper.

GARY   I can never see those things.

KRYSTAL   The constellations? Look, see that trapezium
                sort of shape there?

GARY   The what?

KRYSTAL   The sort of square shape, over there?

GARY   I think so?

KRYSTAL   And those three stars going up at an angle?
                That's the Big Dipper. People always say it
                looks like a saucepan or something, I dunno.
                And those three there, that's Orion's Belt.
                That was the first constellation I learnt. And
                that little cluster of stars there is the Seven
                Sisters.

Gary starts to relax.

GARY   How do you know all of these?

KRYSTAL   I dunno. I just do. I'm not just some bimbo,
                alright. I do know things.

GARY   Sorry.

KRYSTAL   It's alright.

GARY   I just want to know what it's like.

KRYSTAL   To be a constellation?

GARY   To fully be with someone.

KRYSTAL   Oh. We can work on that. Why now though? You've got to be what, 40, 42?

GARY   I'm 31!

KRYSTAL   Sorry. But you must have had loads of opportunity to try it. Why is it only now you wanna do something about it?

           You don't have to tell me. It might just help me to work out what…

GARY   She cheated.

Transition.

HELEN   I did not!

ALEXANDER It was just the story I was telling her. To pity me.

HELEN   But why did she need to pity you? I still don't see why you couldn't have just told her the truth, that you were married, and things had dried up between us!

ALEXANDER   They haven't dried up. Things haven't dried up, have they?

Pause.

HELEN   No. No, of course not. It was just an example of... Let's just get back to it.

ALEXANDER   Ok. Erm... **I told her that my ex cheated on me, and it made me feel crap basically. That was the end of the session.**

What do you actually mean, dried up?

HELEN   Just get on with it.

ALEXANDER   Ok. **The next visit... Actually, I just need a hand from someone for this next scene. Any volunteers? You.**

Alexander speaks to members of the audience, convincing one to join him on stage and convincing them to take a seat in his camping chair.

Just take a seat here. I'll be right back.

Transition.

Krystal stands in the doorway of the caravan looking exhausted. She steps out and takes a seat next to the audience member.

KRYSTAL   That was amazing. You were amazing. Wow. I mean... How was it for you?

The audience member may or may not respond.

> You certainly know your way around a woman don't you?

The audience member may or may not respond.

> Did you get the link through by the way for booking your next appointment? In fact, just wait here a second, I'll go grab you a card with all the details on again. Here, help yourself to a drink too.

Gary enters but freezes as soon as he sees the person in the camping chair. Gary looks at his watch then back at the other person. Gary walks off for a moment before returning, still confused. He offers a hand to the other person to shake.

GARY　　　　　Hello. Gary.

The audience member may or may not reply.

> I thought I must have been early, but only a couple of minutes. Is she still…? Do you mind if I just sit and wait with you? I don't want to intrude if…

Gary sits in the second camping chair.

> Is it just you here? There isn't someone else in with her I mean or have you just…?

The audience member may or may not reply.

>Sorry. I shouldn't ask. None of my business. Sorry.

Beat.

>Lovely night. Not too cold. Or too warm. Just right. What is it you're drinking?

Krystal walks out of caravan and sees the two clients together.

KRYSTAL Sorry about that, I just had to find a card with the right details on. Oh... erm... You're early?

GARY Only by a couple of minutes.

KRYSTAL (*To audience member.*) I'm sorry about this. Here, drop me a message and we'll arrange another appointment.

Krystal ushers off the audience member. Gary tries to shake hands with them again before they go. Gary remains in her camping chair.

GARY They seemed nice. Chatty.

Krystal sits in the other camping chair and chooses a drink from the cooler.

>New regular?

KRYSTAL Why do you still come here, Gary?

GARY What do you mean? You know why.

KRYSTAL It's been three months.

Beat.

> Aside from the occasional kissing session we haven't even tried anything more. I'm not trying to turn you away or anything, I'd just like to know where this is going? Which seems like an odd question under the circumstances I know, but, c'mon. Don't we know each other enough yet for you to get over your little shyness problem?

GARY   I... I don't know. You're kind of putting me on the spot. I don't know.

KRYSTAL   Well, let's find out shall we.

Krystal moves quickly to climb on top of Gary. Krystal kisses Gary passionately, taking him by surprise before he gives in. Krystal stops and slowly pulls her face away from Gary's.

> That seems to have started something.

Gary nods his head, a little embarrassed.

GARY   I can't promise it'll last though.

KRYSTAL   Then let's not waste our chance.

Krystal repositions herself so that her hand is down Gary's trousers. She begins to work.

> How's that?

Gary nods, his breathing now becoming erratic.

>That's it. C'mon. Come on.

Gary's face starts to look different, as if he is concentrating a lot.

>Think of something. Think of something that turns you on. Think of something that gets you off. Your ex. Your favourite porn. C'mon!

GARY   I don't know.

KRYSTAL   Picture the perfect girl. She looks amazing. She's calling you to her. She's wearing... [*Krystal begins describing a member of the audience: their clothes, their hair, their eyes, etc. in as much detail as possible.*] She looks at you, dead in the eye and tells you she wants you.

GARY   Yes?

KRYSTAL   She's calling you.

Gary's face continues to look uncomfortably focused before he seems to give up.

GARY   It's gone. I'm sorry.

Krystal carries on for a second.

KRYSTAL   Stay with me. C'mon, tell me what you wanted her to do to you.

Gary takes a gentle hold of Krystal's wrist, stopping her.

GARY   It's too late.

Krystal retrieves her hand and, deflated, sits in the other camping chair.

          Sorry.

KRYSTAL   What are you apologising for? I'm the one that didn't get you there.

GARY   There was just too much pressure.

KRYSTAL   There's no pressure. I was just trying to be more spontaneous – even less pressure really.

GARY   Not for me. I've had no chance to prepare myself for what might happen. Then, as it happens, I was wondering how far it's going to go. Then I worry that maybe it will go further but I'll lose it. Then once I start to think I'm gonna lose it that's all I can think about and then...

KRYSTAL   You lose it.

GARY   Yeah. I've never been one of these one-night-stand kind of guys. I've got to get to know you first.

Transition.

HELEN   This is one of the bits you were on about at the start isn't it?

ALEXANDER   What do you mean?

HELEN   One of the bits you made up, right? Everything you're about to see is true, except the bits that aren't. This is one of the bits that isn't true, yeah?

Pause.

              Tell me this bit is just for the play, Alex.

ALEXANDER   Course it is. Yeah.

HELEN   Ok. Ok.

Helen returns to her position as Krystal.

ALEXANDER   **You see the problem I have is this block I get if I don't know someone well enough. We were coming up to six months now. How much longer was it gonna take to get to know her. She asked me.**

Transition.

KRYSTAL   How much longer is it gonna take to get to know me?

Transition.

ALEXANDER   **I couldn't tell her. I mean you don't know, do you?**

              I made a suggestion for my next visit. That we just talk. Back to step one, but this time with

49

> a specific topic of conversation. Has anyone
> here heard of the 36 questions?

If someone says yes then Alexander can engage them in conversation to see how much they know.

> Well, there are these 36 questions right which,
> if discussed with a partner, are meant to create
> a really close and intimate bond between you.
> Nothing too fancy, it's just meant to be an
> exercise to get to know someone essentially.
> *The Experimental Generation of
> Interpersonal Closeness: A Procedure
> and Some Preliminary Findings*
> accredited to Dr Arthur Aron and his
> colleagues. For those non academics in here, it
> was also in Cosmo last year, snappily titled 36
> Questions to Fall in Love, and has featured in
> a dozen other magazines before that.

Transition.

The two camping chairs are now positioned to be facing one another. Gary is sitting on one, holding a piece of paper. Krystal is getting herself a drink from inside the caravan before coming out to join Gary, sitting in the opposite chair.

KRYSTAL   So what do we do?

GARY   Just work our way through the questions. You ask a question and we both answer, then

	I ask a question which we both answer, until we've both answered all 36. It was just an idea, that was all.
KRYSTAL	But why? What do you think it's gonna achieve exactly?
GARY	Well, then you know me. And I know you. It might just sort our little problem out and we can try some stuff.
KRYSTAL	So, who goes first?
GARY	You go.
KRYSTAL	Ok. Set 1 slip 1. Given the choice of anyone in the world, whom would you want as a dinner guest?

Pause.

GARY	Now, you answer first since you asked the question, then I'll answer.
KRYSTAL	Oh, erm… Is it living or dead?
GARY	Try not to over think it. Just go for it, first name in your head.
KRYSTAL	Jack the Ripper.
GARY	Why?!

KRYSTAL   Firstly, I think it would be cool to finally know for definite who he was and secondly, he killed a load of my sisters. I think they deserve some vengeance.

GARY   Fair enough.

KRYSTAL   You?

GARY   My grandmother. Before she got ill. She's dead now, but I'd love to have one more meal with her. Hear her stories and her laugh.

KRYSTAL   That's nice.

GARY   Thank you. Slip 2: Would you like to be famous? If so, in what way?

Transition.

ALEXANDER   You get the gist. I'm not going to show you all 36 questions, but I just wanted to share a few of the key ones with you.

HELEN   *We* did this.

ALEXANDER   What?

HELEN   We did this. We did this on like our, fifth date or something.

ALEXANDER   Did we?

HELEN You thought it would be a laugh, so we did it and... and that night was the first time we... Did you actually do this with her?

ALEXANDER Helen.

HELEN Did you?

Silence.

Helen returns to her Krystal position.

Transition.

GARY Slip 8: Name three things you and your partner appear to have in common.

KRYSTAL Shit.

GARY Surely it's not that hard.

Time moves forward.

KRYSTAL Slip 13.

Time moves forward.

That was the first time I properly saw a planet. We looked round the whole sky and he taught me... that's when I learnt the constellations. At the end of the night, when he dropped me back off at home, he gave me the telescope. Said it was mine.

Time moves forward.

GARY   Slip 20: What does friendship mean to you? Trust.

KRYSTAL   That all?

Time moves forward.

GARY   Slip 24.

Time moves forward.

KRYSTAL   Slip 25

Time moves forward.

KRYSTAL   "I wish I had someone with whom I could share…" my life, I guess.

GARY   Yeah?

KRYSTAL   Yeah.

Time moves forward.

GARY   If you were to die this evening with no opportunity to communicate with anyone, what would you most regret not having told someone? Why haven't you told them yet?

Beat.

KRYSTAL   You ok?

Time moves forward.

                Slip 35.

Time moves forward.

GARY	Slip 36: Share a personal problem and ask your partner's advice on how they might handle it. Also, ask your partner to reflect back to you how you seem to be feeling about the problem you have chosen.

KRYSTAL	Wow.

GARY	Yeah. It's the big one.

Beat.

KRYSTAL	Well…

Time moves forward.

Transition.

**ALEXANDER	The final part of the experiment is sustained eye contact. You look into each other's eyes for four minutes.**

Transition.

Krystal and Gary look into each other's eyes. This can last anything up to four minutes but can be shorter. At the end of this time Gary kisses Krystal. Krystal takes Gary by the hand and leads him into the caravan. She turns the lights off and they undress each other. They climb into bed and have sex. Krystal is clearly in charge of the situation, but there is still a gentle and tender quality to the act. It is not romantic, but more than simply platonic. It is affectionate and intimate, but not heated. It is unclear if they both climax or when it happens. They both relax and lay next to each other.

Transition.

Gary climbs out of the bed as if trying not to disturb Krystal and puts on some form of clothing to cover up. This is more due to it being cold rather than any feeling of modesty.

ALEXANDER **So, that happened. It only took me, what, nearly six months.**

HELEN Did you actually sleep with her?

ALEXANDER What?

HELEN You spent six months seeing her and you told me you never did anything more than talk.

ALEXANDER And that's mostly what we did.

HELEN Mostly? You said you never did anything!

ALEXANDER We both agreed it would be better if I got in deep with the research, so that I could write an authentic story.

HELEN We didn't agree to that! You said it. You said you had to experience what it would be like, and *we agreed* that you could meet a sex worker and talk with her.

ALEXANDER And I did.

HELEN   Did you sleep with her?

ALEXANDER   Helen.

HELEN   Answer the fucking question! Did you have sex with a prostitute?

ALEXANDER   We said we'd only refer to them as sex workers.

HELEN   Did you fuck her!?

Silence.

              You just made me act that out. You made me act out your sordid little… it's not even a fantasy! It happened! It actually fucking happened! Even the bits you said didn't, happened!

Silence.

ALEXANDER   It was just the once.

HELEN   What?

ALEXANDER   It didn't mean anything.

HELEN   It doesn't matter if it meant anything or if you only did it once, you shouldn't have done it at all.

Beat.

              You let her jerk you off as well didn't you.

Silence.

        Right. Fuck this.

ALEXANDER   What are you doing?

HELEN   You wanna tell your story, fine, but I'm not being a part of it.

Helen goes to storm off.

ALEXANDER   Helen.

HELEN   No. I'm not doing it. Find yourself another Krystal!

Helen exits.

Alexander looks lost by himself.

ALEXANDER   I presume no one wants to play the part of Krystal for me? No, I guess it would just complicate things. Erm… well, I guess I should finish what I started.

    After that night, I went straight home. I wanted to tell Helen but… I was afraid she might storm off or something. It wasn't just thoughts of guilt around Helen that I was feeling though. I also felt bad for Krystal. For using our interaction as inspiration for this play and her not knowing anything about it. So I booked another meeting. I didn't tell

Helen I booked this appointment. I told her I was... I can't even remember what I told her now.

I told Krystal the truth. That I wasn't Gary. That I was Alexander, a writer, a married writer, and that I was going to write and produce a play that told our story. She was quiet. She was quiet for some time actually. It was the quietest she'd been in all our meetings. She went outside for a minute with her phone. I think she was messaging someone. When she came back in she said she didn't want her story being told. That she'd told me some very personal things and that it wasn't my story to tell. I tried to explain to her that I would of course change names and certain details so people wouldn't know but...

There was a knocking at her door. Turns out her Uncle Stanley's a pretty big chap.

The following lines are directed to specific members of the audience.

Excuse me, could you just help me for a second? Could you just turn those chairs over for me please.

And would you mind just popping inside and throwing the cushions on the floor. Thank you.

> And would you mind just moving all those apart for me, please.

Members of the audience rearrange the set as instructed. As they do this, Alexander asks other members of the audience to touch different parts of his body, asking one to touch his face, one to touch his arms, and wherever else Alexander feels appropriate to invite people to touch. Once touched, Alexander applies purple make-up, possibly even some red liquid until he appears beaten up.

> **Thank you. You can all return to your seats now.**

The caravan now appears wrecked as if a fight has occurred or it has been broken into.

Transition.

Alexander is wandering around outside the caravan, lost, as he looked before. He has clearly been crying. He appears broken. He gets out his mobile phone and tries to call someone. They don't answer. He starts to leave a message...

> It's me. Could you...

...but hangs up before finishing. He waits a minute then sends a text instead.

Helen re-enters the space and sees Alexander. She pities him.

HELEN   You fucking idiot.

ALEXANDER   I didn't think you were coming back.

Alexander gets up.

HELEN   I shouldn't have.

ALEXANDER   I'm sorry.

HELEN   Well, you've done it now, haven't you? You've written your stupid play. We're going to have to do it now.

They stand in the same position as they had at the start.

Are you ready?

Blackout.

A CARAVAN NAMED DESIRE
(THE KRYSTAL SCRIPT)

A Caravan Named Desire – The Krystal Script was first performed as a scripted performance at LCB Depot, Leicester as part of the LCB Performance Week during the 2023 Leicester Comedy Festival.

Gary / Justin Alexander Millington

Krystal Charlotte McKinney

Director Helen Millington

This text was edited following the scripted performance at LCB Depot.

The production was supported using public funding by the National Lottery through Arts Council England. The cast was as follows:

CHARACTERS

GARY / JUSTIN,
early to mid 30s, a little past his best.

KRYSTAL,
older than Gary, looks after herself.

Lines written in bold are directly addressed to the audience. Wherever possible, the audience should be invited to join the conversations with Krystal.

The stage is filled with an old caravan with one side removed so that the audience can see the action within. It has been cared for over the years, but some wear and tear is unavoidable. It looks like it hasn't been moved for a long time. When scenes are exterior to the caravan, they can be performed either in front of the removed wall or the caravan can be rotated. Outside the caravan there are some old camping chairs and a table. Unless otherwise stated, all scenes are at night and the lighting should demonstrate this. The interior of the caravan is lit with old lamps, fairy lights, and one single, bare hanging bulb in the centre of the main living space. The interior of the caravan is surprisingly clean and tidy, though very dated, possibly 80s or early 90s decor. It is cramped, and most of the furniture needs some form of unfolding or setting up.

Gary and Krystal are standing in the caravan. They are looking at each other, both feel a mix of emotions; panic, excitement, nervousness, and fear. They stand in silence for a moment, just staring at each other. She has two suitcases beside her.

GARY	Are you sure you want to do this?

The lights blow and they are left in darkness. Gary and the suitcases disappear in the darkness. Krystal comes forward to the audience.

Transition.

Krystal is tidying up items inside the caravan. Some items she may collect from off stage to put in position. She looks at the audience.

KRYSTAL	**Don't mind me. I'm just getting everything set up.**

She carries on moving some things around before stopping and staring into the audience.

> **I know what you're thinking. Shit! Where's the fucking fourth wall. This bitch could have me doing some kind of interactive shit. Maybe I will. But not much. You see, that's the point of this really. In a way. Trust. You see most of the time you trust the performer not to talk to you, touch you, invite you into the space. This is the space by the way. It's a caravan. Well, it's a set made up to look like a caravan. Again, this is where I need you to trust me, trust the set. Forget that we're currently in the [name**

of space] and believe we're actually outside, and occasionally inside, a caravan. Now, a lot of what you are going to see tonight is true, by which I mean a representation of the truth, of events that have happened.

A dramatisation of real life, real events. Inspired by, based upon. Not exactly a fallacy, more of an interpretation. What I'm trying to say that this is all true, completely true… except the bits that aren't. I swear. Now, before I go any further do we have any questions? Have I said anything that's been unclear at all?

If questions are asked, then Krystal must do her best to answer these questions.

Ok, now that all the formalities are dealt with, onto the story itself. Now, my name is Krystal, that's Krystal with a K by the way, not a C. And this is my home. I'm…well, I'm many things, depending on who I'm talking to. If I'm talking to my mum for instance, I'm manager of a little online shop which sells second hand stuff. If I'm talking to people online, I'm a model and independent film star. If I'm talking to HMRC, then I'm an entertainer. And if I'm talking to you… well, you can make up your own minds I suppose. But what I do isn't the main point of this story, it's more about Gary.

> Now Gary... you know what, this isn't a solo show. I'll just let it get started and come back to you in a bit.

Transition.

Krystal climbs back into the caravan and begins hunting for a light bulb. Once she has found one, she replaces the bulb that blew, and the lights come back on completely red. There is a knocking at the door.

> Just a minute!

Krystal then turns on a lamp with a clear bulb to balance the light. Gary is waiting at the caravan door wearing a cheap-looking button-through shirt and trousers, as if he has just come from work. Everything is a little bit creased, and clearly a little bit old. He knocks again.

> Just a sec!

Krystal turns on some fairy lights that trail around the caravan. She has to click the button a few times to work through the pre-sets before she settles on one. She checks herself in a small mirror before going to the door and opening it.

> Sorry about that, bloody fuse went again. It's always doing it. Are you the new guy Tony was on about? I'll just be a sec. Well, come in.

Gary enters and is directed across to the other end of the caravan. Krystal goes to the bathroom, the only place not entirely visible to

Gary, but is to the audience. Krystal pulls out a small money bag from within the toilet cistern. It contains some notes. She pulls out a few notes and returns the remaining money to where she found it. She returns to Gary.

> I told Tony it was going to be a bit short this month 'cause the internet kept cutting out, so my loss of income is due to him. He knows, he said it's fine so don't you dare say otherwise. Well here, aren't you going to take it?

Krystal thrusts the money towards Gary. Gary, uncertain of what to do, slowly reaches for the money. Before he touches it, Krystal pulls it back.

> Hang on. What's your name again?

GARY   Gary. My name's Gary.

KRYSTAL   You're not the guy Tony said he'd send round.

GARY   Erm… no. I don't know any Tony. I sent you a message last week. We'd arranged to meet.

KRYSTAL   Thursday. We said we'd meet on Thursday. It's not fucking Thursday today is it?

GARY   No. No, it's Wednesday today.

KRYSTAL   We did say Thursday, didn't we?

GARY   Oh yes, we did. I'm early.

KRYSTAL   By twenty-four-fucking-hours. You made me think I'd lost a fucking day or something, Jesus Christ! You don't do that to somebody! Do you have any idea what shit you might have caused by making me think I'd lost a day. I might have plans, very specific plans, you know, which I have to do on a Thursday and now all of a sudden I've lost my Thursday and forgotten to do everything!

GARY   It's not Thursday though, it's Wednesday.

KRYSTAL   I know that now! I knew that five minutes ago. But the time between five minutes ago and now I thought it was fucking Thursday! Fuck me I need a sit down.

GARY   I'm sorry.

Krystal tucks the cash into her clothes.

KRYSTAL   I should think so too. Why are you here anyway?

GARY   I'm sorry. I just, I wanted to make sure I knew the way when I came tomorrow, you know. Make sure I didn't get lost. Or that it wasn't some fake address or something. So, I put the address you gave me into my phone and, as you said, it directed me to this site, and then I saw the caravan and thought, well,

	whilst I'm here I should probably just knock and check it's the right one. I didn't want to come tomorrow and find I was at the wrong door.
KRYSTAL	Right, well… you've found me. Congratulations.
GARY	Thank you.

Beat.

KRYSTAL	Did you want anything else?
GARY	Oh, sorry, no. I just wanted to make sure I knew the way. I should be going actually. Nice to have met you.
KRYSTAL	Wait, wait, wait. Since you're here, do you want to…?
GARY	Oh, no, no thank you. I've got to get back. But I'll definitely be back tomorrow. I'll see myself out.

Gary goes to exit the caravan and closes the door behind him.

KRYSTAL	Alright. Well, see ya.

Transition.

KRYSTAL	**So, that was Gary. A close encounter of, well, the weird kind. I can't say I held out much hope as to whether he would even turn up the**

next night. I couldn't tell if he was serial killer weird or just, you know, weird-weird. Was he going to turn up tomorrow night with a syringe of diamorphine, or a vat of sulphuric acid, or was he more likely to come wearing his granny's knickers and want me to call him Doris? I mean who turns up twenty-four hours early for an appointment just to check they know the way. And who knocks on the door! Either way, he did come back the next day. Though I've got to say, he still didn't fill me with much confidence. I'm glad I took the initial money upfront.

Transition.

Krystal is laid on the sofa bed going through some paperwork. She keeps looking at the clock hanging on the wall. She then taps on her phone to check the time is correct. Gary is outside the caravan, sitting in one of the camping chairs. Eventually, Krystal goes to the caravan door and opens it. She looks about until she spots Gary sitting in the chair and is startled.

KRYSTAL   Creeping Jesus! What the fuck are you doing sat there?!

Gary is startled by her response.

GARY   Sorry. I came to your door, but I was a little early and wasn't sure if you might be busy, so

	I thought I'd just wait out here for a minute. I guess I must have lost track of time.
KRYSTAL	You were meant to have been here at seven.
GARY	I know.
KRYSTAL	It's nine!
GARY	I know. I lost track of time.
KRYSTAL	Fuck me.
GARY	Should I come back another time?
KRYSTAL	No. No, it's fine. I'm charging you as if you were here from seven though.
GARY	Ok.
KRYSTAL	(*to herself.*) Two fucking hours.
GARY	What do we do now then?
KRYSTAL	Do you wanna come in?
GARY	Can do.
KRYSTAL	Unless you wanna do it out here?
GARY	Would you like to?
KRYSTAL	I was kidding. It's fucking freezing out here.
GARY	Sorry.

Beat.

	It's a lovely night.
KRYSTAL	Yeah?

Krystal looks up at the sky.

	Yeah, I suppose it is.
GARY	The moon's so bright.
KRYSTAL	I prefer new moons myself.
GARY	New moons?
KRYSTAL	When there's no moon. You can see the stars better then. The moonlight blocks out a lot of the stars. You're also meant to bow to a new moon and turn over any of your silver for good luck or fortune, or a new love.
GARY	Oh.
KRYSTAL	Well, come on then. I'm letting all the cold in here!

Gary gets up out of the chair and enters the caravan. Krystal shuts the door behind them.

	I can see you're going to be trouble.
GARY	I don't mean to be.
KRYSTAL	I'm sure. You just go from twenty-four hours early to two hours late. What would you have done if someone else turned up?

GARY   Erm... I don't really know. Left, I suppose.

KRYSTAL   Well, you're lucky I'm quiet at the moment. And in a good mood. Look, why don't you take a seat. Do you want a drink?

GARY   Oh, nothing for me, thank you.

KRYSTAL   Then take a seat while I make myself a drink.

Krystal gets a bottle of squash and water out of a cupboard along with a glass and pours herself a drink. She takes a swig then tops up her glass. Gary is looking for somewhere to sit down. He goes to sit on the sofa bed but doesn't want to disturb the papers that are there. He starts to move some of them when Krystal turns around and sees him.

Don't fucking look at those!

Krystal rushes across the caravan and grabs at the papers, piling them up and throwing them in a drawer.

GARY   I'm sorry. I was just trying to find somewhere to sit.

KRYSTAL   So you start looking over my fucking tax returns?

GARY   Tax returns?

Krystal takes Gary by the shoulders and places him on the sofa bed where she has created him a space.

KRYSTAL	Yeah, my fucking tax return. I'm not exactly PAYE doing this, am I? Now, just sit there, and don't move, alright.
GARY	Sorry.
KRYSTAL	And stop apologising.

Gary goes to apologise again but stops himself.

	Now, before we go any further, have you got money?

Gary reaches into his pocket and pulls out his wallet.

GARY	Did it not come through? I used the link you sent me when I booked.
KRYSTAL	That was for one hour. As I said, I'm charging you for three now.
GARY	Oh, yes. Sorry. How much? I've only got…
KRYSTAL	Hang on, let me work it out. Now, you've wasted two hours already, so that's going to be £160. £80 an hour whether we do anything or not, no negotiation. Now, what is it you actually want? You didn't go into much detail before.
GARY	Well…
KRYSTAL	As I said, I'm open to most things but I do have my limits.

GARY   All I really want is…

KRYSTAL   Come on, spit it out.

GARY   Can we just talk?

KRYSTAL   Talk?

GARY   Yeah.

KRYSTAL   I take it back, I will take the money first.

GARY   I'm not saying I definitely don't want to do anything, I'm just not sure that I will.

KRYSTAL   So what *might* you want to do? Hand jobs, blow jobs, vaginal penetration, anal? What?

GARY   I don't know. I probably won't want to try anything. At least not tonight. Maybe if we hit it off we could arrange a second night. I don't really know. I've never done this before. I'm sorry. Maybe I should just go now.

Gary gets up to leave but Krystal stands in his way.

KRYSTAL   £240 and you just wanna talk? Stay for the hour, and we'll talk. That's all that's covered, mind. Anything else happens and I charge more.

GARY   Ok.

Gary gets out his wallet again and takes out some cash.

> I've only got £50 with me.

KRYSTAL   I take card.

Gary takes a card out of his wallet. Krystal picks up her card machine from amongst the paperwork on the bed. There's an awkward silence while Krystal waits for the machine to load. She offers the device to Gary.

> Check the amount and tap.

Gary does so. The transaction goes through. Krystal puts the machine back with the paperwork.

KRYSTAL   Right. So, what do you wanna talk about?

Transition.

KRYSTAL   I hope this isn't breaking up the action too much for you. I don't mean it to, it's just there isn't much point in you watching the next hour when it's just talking. There wasn't even much of that actually, to be fair. There were probably more pauses and silences than talking. And there's no point me making you watch an hour of just pauses and silences. I mean you might as well go and watch a Beckett or a Pinter if you're just gonna watch a silent stage.

Anyway, you didn't miss much. I couldn't even tell you if what we talked about was the truth or not. I mean, he said he worked in one of the offices at the council building in town, but why would you admit to that if you were seeing... someone like me? Then again, I suppose why would you lie about working for the council? In fact, the only thing he told me, which I can be fairly certain is true, was that he was a virgin! Now, I'm not here to judge. People have all sorts of reasons for not wanting to do it. Saving it for marriage. Just not met the right person yet. Not had the opportunity. Mormonism. But Gary, well, who knows! I like to treat a person's virginity, or at least their first sexual experiences, like a game of Cluedo. Me for example: Ms Morris's Grandson, behind the cinema, with his fingers. Never got his name. Clive Sinclair, inside my Dad's shed, from behind. I still come over all funny when I get the smell of creosote. Mr Wallace, on the back seat of his Toyota Corolla, wearing his wife's knickers. Him, not me. That was my first paid job. I make it sound as if I've never had it 'normal'. A loving boyfriend, on the bed, missionary. It's just not as exciting to talk about really, is it?

Now, as I think I said, Gary and I didn't do anything on that first visit. We didn't do anything for his first three visits! The talking got a little better. But it was still just small

talk. It was on his fourth visit however when things started to get a little bit more interesting.

Transition.

Gary is pacing around outside the caravan. Krystal is standing at the door as before trying to convince him to come in.

KRYSTAL   Look, the longer you stay out here the colder my caravan's going to get and then we'll both be complaining. Now, why don't you just get in here and tell me what's shit in your bloody pants today?

GARY   Nothing's shit in my pants!

Gary storms into the caravan. Krystal moves out the way before he can push past her.

        Do you like me?

KRYSTAL   Do I what?

GARY   Do you like me?

KRYSTAL   To be honest you're creeping me out a little bit.

GARY   I know you don't like me like me, that's not what I'm asking. Do you... do you think I'm an alright person.

KRYSTAL   I've only met you a handful of times and even then you barely speak, so I can't really say. I doubt you're a complete wanker if that's what you mean?

GARY   Ok.

KRYSTAL   I'm not saying I've completely ruled it out, mind.

GARY   I think I like you.

KRYSTAL   Right.

GARY   Not, like that. I could never like you like that.

KRYSTAL   Good to know.

GARY   I don't mean it like that. I just mean, I like you as a person, an acquaintance, sort of.

Beat.

I don't think you're a complete wanker either.

They both smile. This is the first time they both seem relaxed.

KRYSTAL   Look, why don't you take a seat, I'll make us both a drink and we can have a chat again.

Krystal turns to get some cans of drink out of her cupboard. Gary just stands and stares at her.

GARY   I want to do more than just talk tonight.

Krystal turns to look at him.

></p>

                If that's ok.

KRYSTAL   Erm. Sure. Yeah. What did you have in mind?

GARY   I don't know.

KRYSTAL   Right.

GARY   I just… I want to try something new.

Pause.

KRYSTAL   Alright. I'll get those drinks.

Krystal gets out some cups to pour the drinks into but changes her mind.

GARY   I don't drink.

KRYSTAL   I get the impression you're going to need something. It's only coke anyway.

GARY   Can I just have a water?

KRYSTAL   Alright.

Krystal fills his glass with water and takes it over to him. Gary just watches her, not thinking to take the glass from her. Krystal just places it on the side. He takes a step toward her as if about to do something but is unsure what. He takes a step back, sees the water and takes a mouthful.

GARY	Do you kiss?
KRYSTAL	Kiss?
GARY	I know some…
KRYSTAL	Some?
GARY	What do you like to be called?
KRYSTAL	Krystal.
GARY	I mean…
KRYSTAL	I know what you mean. I'm Krystal.
GARY	Well, I just know some… Krystals that don't kiss.
KRYSTAL	Know many Krystals do you?
GARY	Well, no. No, I mean I've heard, or rather seen on TV, that some don't like to kiss.

KRYSTAL	Do you like to kiss?

Gary doesn't know how to respond for a second before eventually nodding.

	Then we can kiss.
GARY	Ok. Ok.

Gary moves close to Krystal again, moving in to kiss her.

Transition.

KRYSTAL His hands were all over me. His fingers running through my hair, pulling my face into his. I felt his fingers slowly run down my back before grabbing my arse. Our bodies rubbing together, my tits pressed up against him. I could feel him throbbing against me, wanting me, wanting to do things to me! He ripped open my top, pushed me to the bed, undid his trousers and go it out! His massive cock in his hands, me in his eyes and his mind on one thing… I'm just kidding you. Can you seriously imagine him…? We just kissed. But, you know what, he wasn't too bad. Better than I expected. Good even, actually. Eventually. A little awkward and tentative to start with but he began to get into after a while. It was a bit like being back in school. Remember, with your first boyfriends or girlfriends, you'd spend literally minutes kissing and it felt like you'd done so much.

Who here remembers the name of their first kiss by the way, you don't need to call it out, just a show of hands. Everyone remembers their first. Ok, a little trickier now. Who remembers the name of their first kissed? Ok. Keep your hands up. Who remembers *how*

many people they've kissed, the actual number, not a round abouts? So, we're not really all that different are we. Some of us, anyway. Dale was mine. Dale McDermott. This geeky little twerp who fancied me in primary school. I just wanted to see what he'd do if I did it. Ran up to him, grabbed him, I mean properly grabbed him and planted one on his lips then ran off again. He hit the floor like a sack of spuds. Apparently he hit his head and had to go to A&E, but that was just school gossip, who knows really.

Transition.

Gary is sitting on the sofa bed. Krystal is in the kitchen area making herself another drink.

KRYSTAL   So be honest, was that your first kiss?

Gary seems to be just staring off into the middle distance, holding his glass of water.

GARY   No. Erm… Year 5. Selena French, at St Mary's Primary School. Kiss chase in the courtyard. I didn't even know I was playing but she just ran up to me, grabbed me, I mean properly grabbed me, and just planted one on my lips then ran off.

KRYSTAL   Did she kiss you as her name suggests?

GARY   Pardon?

KRYSTAL   French?

GARY   We were only nine.

KRYSTAL   D'you want me to relieve you of your glass?

Gary doesn't respond.

KRYSTAL   You alright?

Gary shakes his head.

GARY   I lied to you, *Krystal*.

Transition.

KRYSTAL   Lies aren't anything new. If anything, it's expected. It's unusual if they don't lie to be honest. I mean let's face it, if you were given the chance to be anyone you want to be, which is basically what's on offer here isn't it? The chance to be whoever you want to be. Make your dreams come true. Even if it's just for an hour or two. Why would you be yourself? But I wasn't expecting him to say what he told me next.

Transition.

GARY   I've been seeing someone.

KRYSTAL   Ok.

GARY   I'm not anymore!

KRYSTAL   Right.

GARY   But it was pretty serious.

KRYSTAL   Ok.

GARY   I just thought you should know.

KRYSTAL   Hey, I'm not here to judge. Plenty of the people come to see me after a relationship. Hell, plenty see me when they're still in a relationship. That's nothing new.

GARY   It's just…

KRYSTAL   Hang on, does this mean you're not a virgin?

GARY   Well, not exactly.

KRYSTAL   Well you either are or you're not. Either way, it doesn't really bother me. You can say what you want, you're paying for the time.

GARY   It's just, I'm a virgin in terms of… I've never really fully been with a woman.

KRYSTAL   What do you mean?

GARY   I'm… well, I struggle.

KRYSTAL   Right.

GARY   To keep it up.

Beat.

> You see, I've always fancied women, it's not like I'm gay or anything but whenever we start to get down to it I get... nervous. I always try to put it off as long as I can but eventually the question comes, and it all gets a little awkward.

Beat.

> It's not like I don't enjoy it. I love the build-up, the foreplay and everything but I've got to keep the focus on them, anything that relies on me to be... hard... just puts the pressure all back on me. It's the same with just kissing. I always have to let them make the first move.

KRYSTAL   Like Selena.

GARY   Yeah.

KRYSTAL   Ok. So when you say you're a virgin, you mean... what?

GARY   I've never... actually... finished with a girl. Woman. I've started out alright, but I've never got to the actual...

KRYSTAL   Cumming?

GARY   No.

Beat.

KRYSTAL   But you do when you wank right? You do wank don't you?

Silence.

GARY   Erm... Do you mind if I just take a minute? I'm just getting a bit... sorry.

Gary rushes outside of the caravan to try and catch his breath. Krystal stands at the door of the caravan and watches him.

KRYSTAL   You alright?

GARY   No. I get like this. I don't really know why I'm here. I don't know what's wrong with me.

KRYSTAL   It's alright, just take a breath. Nothing's wrong with you. You want another water or something?

GARY   No, I'll be alright. I just need...

Gary sits down on one of the camping chairs again. He looks up at the sky.

You're right. You can see more stars without the moon.

Krystal steps out of the caravan and looks up.

KRYSTAL   Beautiful, isn't it? If you look behind you you'll see the Big Dipper.

GARY   I can never see those things.

KRYSTAL   The constellations? Look, just turn around. See that trapezium sort of shape there?

GARY   The what?

KRYSTAL   The sort of square shape, over there?

GARY   I think so?

KRYSTAL   And those three stars going up at an angle? That's the Big Dipper.

GARY   Oh, ok.

KRYSTAL   People always say it looks like a saucepan or something, I dunno. And those three there, that's Orion's Belt. That was the first constellation I learnt.

Gary starts to relax.

GARY   I just want to know what it's like.

KRYSTAL   What what's like?

GARY   To fully be with someone.

KRYSTAL   Oh. We can work on that. Why now though? You've got to be what, 40, 42?

GARY   I'm 30!

KRYSTAL	Sorry. But you must have had loads of opportunity to try it. Why is it only now you wanna do something about it?

Beat.

You don't have to tell me. It might just help me to work out what...

GARY	She cheated.
KRYSTAL	Who?
GARY	Rachel. She kept asking if it was something she was doing or if I didn't find her attractive or something, but I kept putting it off and I didn't know how to tell her.

Beat.

I went round to her's one evening and she was just sat on the sofa crying. I thought something awful had happened to her, I tried to console her but then she told me she couldn't be with me any longer. She said I was making her feel unattractive and making her doubt herself and I didn't want that, of course I didn't. I tried to suggest that we went to counselling or maybe we should try spicing things up a bit, without sex.

Transition.

KRYSTAL   This went on for some time so I'm just going to cut to the end bit. It's the only key bit really.

Transition.

GARY   But it came down to just accepting that I was never gonna have sex or just find a way of getting it over with for the first time. So I thought what better way than to do it simply as a transaction. No emotion. Just business.

KRYSTAL   But we still haven't done it so that hasn't worked.

GARY   No. You see I've never been one of these one-night stand kinds of people. I still need to feel some connection, even if I'm not meant. Like this. I mean, no offence, but that's why I thought this would be the best way to do it. No connection, no feeling, just…sex. I know what I'm like, I fall easily. At least this way, even if I started to get feelings for you, you won't reciprocate. I mean, why would you? I just need to do it once to know how it feels, but I know I won't be able to do it unless we build up to it, try a few things first. Like it's a real relationship, but I know it's now.

KRYSTAL   So you're after the Girlfriend Experience?

GARY   Sort of, I guess, but, not that at the same time. I don't want you to treat me like a boyfriend or anything. This is just what it is.

KRYSTAL   How long were you with Rachel?

GARY   Four months. We'd done some stuff, but it was just hands and mouths and stuff. Mainly me doing it to her. Even if she tried to give me a blowy I'd panic and quickly turn it back on her. As soon as I start to think about it, it just… goes. And then I'm just not in the mood. And now I'm worrying that what if I just don't like it, then what?

Krystal looks at her watch. Time is up.

KRYSTAL   You're over thinking all of this. Just get a plan together and go for it!

GARY   I can't do a plan. If I have a plan and something goes wrong then I'll just worry about that.

KRYSTAL   Spontaneity then.

GARY   Maybe if I got some Viagra or something. We could definitely do it then.

KRYSTAL   That's certainly one way to do it, but I'm afraid…

GARY   You can get it over the counter now. And online.

KRYSTAL   Well, have a think about it.

Gary is not taking the hint to leave.

GARY   Could we just try a kiss again. See if I feel anything.

KRYSTAL   Maybe next time.

GARY   Next time?

KRYSTAL   I've got another…

GARY   Another what?

KRYSTAL   Your times up. I've got another appointment.

GARY   Oh. Sorry. I didn't realise. You should have said.

KRYSTAL   Next time. We'll see what's gonna be best for you.

GARY   Ok. I'll book it when I get home. Same time work for you?

KRYSTAL   Yes. Yeah, that's fine. Please, though, if you wouldn't mind. I've really got to get ready.

GARY   Oh. Yes. Of course. Sorry.

Gary makes his way off. He looks back at Krystal.

You can just tell me to shut up by the way. I don't normally talk all that much with new people. I guess you make me feel at ease. Comfortable.

Krystal smiles.

KRYSTAL   See you next time.

Gary exits. As soon as he's out of sight, Krystal, starts tidying up the caravan: making the bed, putting the mugs away. She pulls out a cooler of canned drinks. The cooler contains a variety of soft drinks and water. Krystal places the cooler between the two camping chairs at the front.

Transition.

I do hate a rush. I'm self-employed for a reason. I can stick to my own schedule, I don't have to answer to anyone, so as soon as someone starts fucking with my schedule I quickly start to lose my shit. Time is money, as they say. I can't be the only one like that.

Show of hands, who uses an alarm to wake you up? Do you snooze it though? Alarm set for six but don't get up till seven sort of thing? I can't do that. I set the alarm - I get up with that alarm. I have to. You do if you're your own boss. I have a very strict routine otherwise I never get anything done. Up at eight. Get tidied

up from the night before. Breakfast at eight-thirty. Nine o'clock, time to work. I check over my day in my diary, see if any orders have come through over-night, (*she picks up some women's knickers from a dirty clothes basket and puts them in envelopes*) package up anything that needs packing, put on anything that needs putting on for new orders. Then create some online, I won't show you that just now.

Evenings and nights vary from day to day. I've got my regulars, like anyone. Clive's nice. Tuesday evenings, seven-thirty. He's a young widow, fifties I think. He just gets lonely, and I think Tuesday used to be his regular with his wife. Then there's the three Ms: Matt, Matty and Matthew. They're all Friday night. One after the other. Then there are semi-regulars. Once a fortnight or once a month-ers. Occasionals and of course one-offs and new clients. I usually try and have Sundays and Mondays off for general admin but depending on how the month's going I might take the odd bit of work here and there. It is a full-time job doing this.

Krystal opens the cooler and makes it clear to the audience what is inside.

> Anyone want a drink by the way? It's just soft drinks. I don't keep alcohol in. Obvious potential issues. Well, I say obvious, it wasn't always obvious. But hey, you live and learn I guess. Seriously though, anyone want one?

Krystal hands some drinks out to people, one of whom she invites to sit in one of the camping chairs.

> Is that comfortable enough for you? Are you alright there? I'm just going to quickly grab something.

Krystal goes back inside the caravan, leaving the audience member in the chair.

> **I'll just be a second!**

Transition.

Gary enters but freezes as soon as he sees the person in the camping chair. Gary looks at his watch then back at the other person. Gary walks off for a moment before returning, still confused. He offers a hand to the other person to shake.

GARY   Hello. Gary.

The audience member may or may not reply.

> I thought I must have been early, but I'm not. Not really. Just a couple of minutes. Is

> she...? Do you mind if I just sit and wait with you? I don't want to intrude if...

Gary sits in the second camping chair.

> Is it just you here? There someone else in with her I mean or have you just...?

The audience member may or may not reply.

> Sorry. I shouldn't ask. None of my business. Sorry.

Beat.

> Lovely night. Not too cold. Or too warm. Just right. What is it you're drinking?

Krystal walks out of caravan and sees the two clients together.

KRYSTAL   Sorry about that, I just had to find a card with the correct details on. Oh...erm. Sorry, you're early?

GARY   Only five minutes.

KRYSTAL   I'm sorry about this. Here, drop me a message and we'll arrange another appointment.

Krystal ushers off the audience member. Gary tries to shake hands with them again before they go. Gary remains in his camping chair.

GARY   They seemed nice. Chatty.

Krystal sits in the other camping chair and chooses a drink from the cooler.

                New regular?

KRYSTAL   Why do you still come here, Gary?

GARY   What do you mean? You know why.

KRYSTAL   It's been three months.

Beat.

                Aside from the occasional kissing session we haven't even tried anything more. I'm not trying to turn you away or anything, I'd just like to know where this is going? Which seems like an odd question under the circumstances I know, but, c'mon. Don't we know each other enough yet for you to get over your little shyness problem?

GARY   I... I don't know. You're kind of putting me on the spot. I don't know.

KRYSTAL   Well, let's find out shall we.

Krystal moves quickly to climb on top of Gary. Krystal kisses Gary passionately, taking him by surprise before he gives in. Krystal stops and slowly pulls her face away from Gary's.

KRYSTAL   That seems to have started something.

Gary nods his heads, a little embarrassed.

GARY I can't promise it'll last though.

KRYSTAL Then let's not waste our chance.

Krystal repositions herself so that her hand is down Gary's trousers. She begins to work.

KRYSTAL How's that?

Gary nods, his breathing now becoming erratic.

> That's it. C'mon. Come on.

Gary's face starts to look different, as if he is concentrating a lot.

> Think of something. Think of something that turns you on. Think of something that gets you off. Rachel. Another ex. Your favourite porn. C'mon!

GARY I don't know.

KRYSTAL Picture the perfect girl. She looks amazing. She's calling you to her. She wearing... [*Krystal begins describing a member of the audience: their clothes, their hair, their eyes, etc. in as much detail as possible.*] She looks at you, dead in the eye and tells you she wants you.

GARY Yes?

KRYSTAL She is calling you.

Gary's face continues to look uncomfortably focused before he seems to give up.

GARY   It's gone. I'm sorry.

Krystal carries on for a second.

KRYSTAL   Stay with me. C'mon, tell me what you want her to do to you.

Gary takes a gentle hold of Krystal's wrist, stopping her.

GARY   It's too late.

Krystal retrieves her hand and, deflated, sits in the other camping chair.

GARY   Sorry.

KRYSTAL   What are you apologising for? I'm the one that didn't get you there.

GARY   There was just too much pressure.

KRYSTAL   There's no pressure. I was just trying to be more spontaneous – even less pressure really.

GARY   Not for me. I've had no chance to prepare myself for what might happen. Then as it happens I was wondering how far it's going to go. Then I worry that maybe it will go further but I'll lose it. Then once I start to think I'm gonna lose it that's all I can think about and then…

KRYSTAL   You lose it.

GARY   Yeah.

Transition.

KRYSTAL   **You know what, I've got to say I was pleasantly surprised by his honesty. I mean let's face it, how many men would admit they struggle to get it up or have ever struggled. Most men would say they haven't. Or no comment of course.**

Have you ever struggled to get it up with someone sir? (*She doesn't give time for a response.*) **See, no response, men don't like that question, or rather, they don't like the truth behind the answer to that question.**

You see the problem with Gary was this block he had if he didn't know you well enough. We were coming up to sixth months now. What more did he need to know? Tell you what, credit to Rachel for sticking with him for four months. I'd have jacked him in way sooner. How much longer was it gonna take to get to know me. I asked him.

Transition.

How much longer is it gonna take to get to know me?

Transition.

He couldn't tell me. I mean you don't know do you!

I made a suggestion for his next visit. That we just talk. Back to step one, but this time with a specific topic of conversation. Has anyone here heard of the 36 questions?

If someone says yes then Krystal can engage them in conversation to see how much they know.

Well, there are these 36 questions right which, if discussed with a partner, is meant to create a really close and intimate bond between you. Nothing too fancy, it's just meant to be an exercise to get to know someone essentially. *The Experimental Generation of Interpersonal Closeness: A Procedure and Some Preliminary Findings* accredited to Dr Arthur Aron and his colleagues. An experiment on interpersonal closeness through this set of questions. For those non academics in here, it was also in Cosmo last year, snappily titled 36 Questions to Fall in Love, and probably featured a dozen times before that.

Transition.

The two camping chairs are now positioned to be facing one another. Gary is sitting on one, holding a piece of paper. Krystal is getting herself a drink from inside the caravan before coming out to join Gary, sitting in the opposite chair.

GARY	So what do we do?
KRYSTAL	Just work our way through the questions. You ask a question and we both answer, then I ask a question which we both answer, until we've both answered all 36. We've got to be honest though.
GARY	And then what?
KRYSTAL	Well, then you know me. And I know you. It might just sort our little problem out.
GARY	Oh. Ok.
KRYSTAL	Unless you don't want to sort it out?
GARY	No, no. I do.

Silence for a moment.

KRYSTAL	Do you want to leave it for tonight.
GARY	No, no. You've gone to all this trouble.
KRYSTAL	I've only printed off some questions.

GARY   There's only silence waiting for me at home. I'd rather be here to be honest.

KRYSTAL   Ok.

GARY   So who goes first?

KRYSTAL   You go.

GARY   Ok. Set 1 slip 1. Actually, before we start, there is one thing I'd like to ask.

KRYSTAL   Yeah?

GARY   Krystal? Is that really your name?

KRYSTAL   It's how I like to be referred to.

GARY   But were you born Krystal?

KRYSTAL   Are any of us born…

GARY   Never mind. I just wondered that was all. It doesn't matter. Set 1, slip 1…

KRYSTAL   Edith.

GARY   What?

KRYSTAL   My mum called me Edith. After Edith Piaf.

GARY   As in *No Regrets* lady?

KRYSTAL   Yes. Ironic, right?

GARY   Edith.

KRYSTAL   Don't.

GARY   I think it suits…

KRYSTAL   No it doesn't. And it's not the name I chose at birth, and it's not the name I choose now, alright?

GARY   Ok.

KRYSTAL   Start us off then.

GARY   Ok. Slip 1: Given the choice of anyone in the world, whom would you want as a dinner guest?

Pause.

KRYSTAL   Now, you answer first since you asked the question, then I'll answer.

GARY   Oh, erm… Is it living or dead?

KRYSTAL   Try not to over think it. Just go for, first name in your head.

GARY   My grandmother. Before she got ill. She's dead now, but I'd love to have one more meal with her. Hear her stories and her laugh.

KRYSTAL   That's nice.

GARY   Thank you. You?

KRYSTAL   Jack the Ripper.

GARY   Why?!

KRYSTAL   Firstly, I think it would be cool to finally know for definite who he was and secondly, he killed a load of my sisters. I think they deserve some vengeance.

GARY   Fair enough.

KRYSTAL   Slip 2: Would you like to be famous? If so, in what way?

Beat.

GARY   Is it me first?

KRYSTAL   No, I was just thinking. I don't think I would. I would like to be successful, but not famous.

GARY   Successful at what?

KRYSTAL   This. I enjoy my job. I know it's not everyone's ideal career, but I enjoy it and it makes me money. I'd love to be one of those girls you see on TikTok or The Sun online or whatever saying they quit their job now they earn half a million a week by selling pictures of themselves doing something stupid in lingerie. I'd like to be earning that much, but I think my days of getting that much, with this body are long gone. Fame just comes with too many add-ons, like losing your anonymity and stuff. Nah, just money and recognition is enough for me.

GARY   I'd love to be famous.

KRYSTAL   Yeah?

GARY   Yeah. Have people around you all the time. Telling you you're great and congratulating you on everything you do.

KRYSTAL   But what would you do?

GARY   Erm... I don't really know I guess. Can't really get famous by working at the council can you? Maybe a model? I know I couldn't be one, but if we're playing hypotheticals, why not?

Transition.

KRYSTAL   **You get the gist. I'm not going to show you all 36 questions, but I just wanted to share a few of the key ones with you.**

Transition.

Time moves forward.

KRYSTAL   Slip 8: Name three things you and your partner appear to have in common.

GARY   Shit.

KRYSTAL   It's not that hard.

Time moves forward.

> Slip 13: If a crystal ball could tell you the truth about yourself, your life, the future, or anything else, what would you want to know?

Time moves forward.

GARY   How about you? What is your most treasured memory?

Krystal thinks for a minute.

KRYSTAL   When I was five, my neighbour used to take me out over to the green at the edge of town so we could see the stars. Too much light pollution in the town itself so we had to drive out a little bit. One night he said he had something to show me and when we pulled up he opened the boot of his car and in there he had this telescope. It looked absolutely massive, but I'm probably just remembering it that way. That was the first time I properly saw a planet. We looked round the whole sky and he taught me... that's when I learnt the constellations. At the end of the night, when he dropped me back off at home, he gave me the telescope. Said it was mine. He said he was moving away and wouldn't have any space for it and knew it would go to good use with me.

Time moves forward.

Slip 20: What does friendship mean to you? Trust.

GARY   That all?

KRYSTAL   If you have trust, what more do you need?

GARY   I guess so. I mean I still want trust, but I also need a sense of humour, good conversation, likes going out for meals or coming and going round each other's houses to chill.

KRYSTAL   You make it sound like you want a date with everyone you know.

GARY   I just wanna know we have things in common and will deffo get on.

KRYSTAL   'Deffo get on'?

GARY   What? I'm street.

They both laugh.

Time moves forward.

KRYSTAL   Complete this sentence: "I wish I had someone with whom I could share…" my life, I guess.

GARY   Yeah?

KRYSTAL   Yeah. I know this career doesn't scream girlfriend material, but I'd like to meet someone someday who gets me and wants to be with me. I'd probably stop meeting up with and actually having sex with guys, but I could still do the internet stuff. I just need to find someone who gets me and will let me be who I want to be.

GARY   I get you.

KRYSTAL   Thanks. How about you?

GARY   I wish I had someone with whom I could share… everything.

KRYSTAL   Everything?

GARY   Yeah, everything. All my secrets and worries and fears and dreams and…well, everything.

Time moves forward.

GARY   If you were to die this evening with no opportunity to communicate with anyone, what would you most regret not having told someone? Why haven't you told them yet?

Beat.

KRYSTAL   You ok?

Time moves forward.

        Slip 36: Share a personal problem and ask your partner's advice on how they might handle it. Also, ask your partner to reflect back to you how you seem to be feeling about the problem you have chosen.

GARY   Wow.

KRYSTAL   Yeah. It's the big one.

Beat.

        Well...

GARY   She cheated on me.

Krystal stays quiet.

        The night I found her crying and said how I made her feel... she also said she found someone he made her feel good about herself again and... they slept together. She said... she said she didn't regret it, she just regretted doing it before she ended it with me. I never want to make anyone feel like that again. I want to be the one who makes them feel good. How can I do that if I can't give them this?

Transition.

KRYSTAL	The final part of the experiment is sustained eye contact. You look into each other's eyes for four minutes.

Transition.

Krystal and Gary look into each other's eyes. This can last anything up to four minutes but can be shorter. At the end of this time Gary kisses Krystal. Krystal takes Gary by the hand and leads him into the caravan. She turns the lights off and they undress each other. They climb into bed and have sex. Krystal is clearly in charge of the situation, but there is still a gentle and tender quality to the act. It is not romantic, but more than simply platonic. It is affectionate and intimate, but not heated. It is unclear if they both climax or when it happens. They both relax and lay next to each other.

Transition.

Krystal climbs out of the bed as if trying not to disturb Gary and puts on some form of clothing to cover up. This is more due to it being cold rather than any feeling of modesty. During this speech we see Gary dress himself and walk out of the caravan as if avoiding Krystal.

KRYSTAL	So, that happened. It only took him, what, just over six months? Longer than he was with Rachel, shorter than a Victorian engagement. Be honest, who thought we'd actually even get to this stage? (*If members of the audience don't raise their hands, ask why not.*) **And you know**

> what, he actually wasn't that bad to be fair. I mean I've certainly had worse, that's for sure.
>
> When we finished we both got dressed and he left. It was the first time he ever left without saying he would book another visit. Now don't get me wrong, I know the whole point of the visits was for him to build up to having sex, but I was surprised how cold he became. Almost instantly. I half expected to get a booking or something saying he wanted to meet but… I'm not bothered. Just surprised. I just got used to our evenings of chatting and what not. Actually, I tell a lie, I did get one thing. Just over a week after we had sex I got a package.

Krystal runs inside and grabs a book from under her pillow. She comes back out with it. It's a copy of 'Turn Left at Orion'.

> This arrived. No note or anything but I can only think it was from Gary. It's a guidebook for the stars and the night sky. Just a little something to say thank you I guess. I've never been given a gift before from a client. It's sweet.
>
> A year went by. Nothing much changed. Gained some new customers, lost some others. The three Ms became two as Matt moved away to work in the city. Oh, and Clive met a new

> lady. He booked one last visit just to let me know, which was sweet. He showed me a picture. Susan, I think he said her name was. Looked like a bit of a God botherer, but if it's what keeps him happy.
>
> I've got a new guy, started about four weeks ago maybe.
>
> (*To a single audience member.*) I'm sorry, could you please just touch an area of my face. Anywhere you like.

Wherever the audience member touches on Krystal's face, Krystal will then touch it herself.

> Thank you.
>
> (*Back to everyone.*) He says his name's Kian, but there's something about him... I don't know. I'm just always a little on edge when he's here. I don't think he's drunk when he comes round but he certainly doesn't *not* smell of booze.

Krystal begins to apply purple make up to where the audience member touched her.

> And he clearly smokes. I can smell it on his hair when he climbs on stop of me. And he's not gentle. I dunno.

Then I got a message through. A booking. Gary. It took me by surprise. It was the same day and time as he always had before. And as he always had been before, he was early.

Transition.

Gary enters, looks at his watch, looks at the caravan door, then moves to sit in his usual camping chair. Krystal pops her head around the door.

KRYSTAL   I knew you'd be early.

Krystal steps out of the caravan and approaches Gary who stands up to greet her. He notices her black eye.

GARY   What happened?

KRYSTAL   New client. It's alright, he won't be coming back. Every job has its drawbacks.

GARY   Have you been to the hospital?

KRYSTAL   Nah, don't be soft. I put some peas on it. It'll be fine. It's better than it was. Anyway, what are you doing here?

GARY   I wanted to see you.

KRYSTAL   I gathered that much.

GARY   I wanted to apologise.

KRYSTAL   For what?

GARY   For ending things like I did.

KRYSTAL   Hey, it's fine. It's not like we were together or anything. You came for sex. You got it. Why hang around?

GARY   We were friends.

Silence.

Krystal doesn't know how to respond but looks as if she's about to cry. She turns to hide her face.

KRYSTAL   You want a drink or anything?

GARY   I didn't mean for things to end that way. I should have contacted you.

KRYSTAL   I've got squashes, tea, coffee. You know, the usual.

GARY   When I went home that night I… I contacted Rachel. I told her that I was sorry for how I made her feel and that I had gotten over my problem, that I'd been seeing someone to help and that I was all sorted now. I told her I still had feelings for her and that I wanted to make things right.

KRYSTAL   What did she say?

Beat.

GARY	That it didn't matter. That's she'd already moved on.
KRYSTAL	Oh. Sorry.
GARY	Thank you. But it's ok. I didn't mind. I was actually relieved, in a way. It was as if a part of me wanted to get her back and prove to her that it wasn't her fault, but there was a part of me that didn't actually want to be with her because I had feelings for someone else.
KRYSTAL	Who?
GARY	You.
KRYSTAL	Well, I see why you didn't message then. You didn't want feelings for me. I mean if you carried on seeing me then you obviously would have just fallen madly in love with me or something.
GARY	They weren't those feelings. I liked you. I liked your company. I wanted to spend time with you as a friend.

Beat.

KRYSTAL	I'd have liked that.

Beat.

GARY	Did you get the book?

KRYSTAL   Yes.

GARY   I was gonna put a note with it to try and explain but I didn't know what to write.

KRYSTAL   I knew it was from you. Thank you.

GARY   I wanted to give it to you myself.

KRYSTAL   That would have been nice.

GARY   But I was afraid I'd already left it too long. Then once I started building it up in my head I started to have a panic attack and then I just…

KRYSTAL   No, of course.

Beat.

GARY   I'm sorry.

Beat.

KRYSTAL   So have you been seeing anyone else yet?

GARY   A couple of people.

KRYSTAL   Wow. One fuck and you're a proper little player now.

GARY   Hardly. Nothing particularly serious but I have managed to go a bit further now. You helped with that.

KRYSTAL   It's just confidence.

GARY   That you gave me. Are you sure that eye's alright?

KRYSTAL   Yeah, trust me, it looks worse than it is.

Beat.

GARY   I've thought about you a lot over the past year.

KRYSTAL   Yeah?

GARY   Every time I've watched the stars it makes me think of you. I've actually taken up a bit of star gazing myself recently. I decided I needed a hobby. Get me out more. Even got my own little telescope.

KRYSTAL   Yeah?.

Beat.

                Well, I suppose you've booked the hour now, so we'll have to get on with it.

GARY   What's up?

KRYSTAL   Nothing. What do you actually want to do then? Are we just talking, star gazing or do you want to fuck again?

GARY   Krystal?

KRYSTAL	What? You're the one who just spent the last five minutes saying how much you thought we were friends after just leaving without saying goodbye and now are too scared to just come and see me without booking an appointment. Are we friends or are you a customer 'cause I need to know how we're doing this now.
GARY	I...
KRYSTAL	In fact, wait here.

Krystal goes to the toilet cistern and gets out the money. She takes out a few notes, returns the toilet back to how it was, and then goes back to Gary.

	Here. Here's a refund for tonight. I forgot. I've got to get a load of stuff ready for the post tomorrow morning.
GARY	Krystal.
KRYSTAL	Sorry, I really should have blocked it out on my calendar. It's my fault. Don't worry about it.
GARY	I'll book for another time then.
KRYSTAL	I'm really busy at the moment. I'll have to see.

Krystal makes her way back into the caravan, leaving Gary alone.

GARY   I'll see you soon.

Gary waits for a moment then leaves. After a moment, Krystal comes back out, looking after him.

Transition.

Krystal approaches members of the audience.

KRYSTAL   **Excuse me, could you just help me for a second? Could you just turn those chairs over for me please. And would you mind just popping inside and ripping those off and flipping that over onto its side. Thank you. And would you mind just sticking some of this tape over that for me please.**

Members of the audience rearrange the set as instructed. As they do this, Krystal asks other members of the audience to touch different parts of her body, asking one to touch her face, one to touch her arms, and wherever else Krystal feels like inviting people to touch. Once touched, Krystal applies the same purple make-up, as before, and possibly even some red liquid until she appears beaten up.

                        Thank you. You can return to your seats now.

The caravan now appears wrecked as if a fight has occurred or it has been broken into.

Transition.

Krystal is sitting on the step of the caravan with pieces of furniture and broken items all around her. The bed sheets have been torn off the bed. The pillows are on the floor. The toilet cistern has been removed. She has clearly been crying. She appears broken. She gets out her mobile phone and tries to call someone. They don't answer. She starts to leave a message...

KRYSTAL   It's me. Could you...

...but hangs up before finishing. She waits a minute then sends a text instead.

Transition.

Krystal approaches the audience as she has done before as if about to speak but stops. She goes inside the caravan and pulls out a bottle of whiskey which has been hidden somewhere. She drinks from the bottle.

Transition.

Krystal returns to sitting on the step of the caravan with the whiskey bottle. After a short time Gary appears.

GARY   Oh Christ! What happened? Are you alright?

KRYSTAL   I knew I didn't trust him. I knew he was a bad'un but I thought I'd be alright.

GARY   Who? Have you called police?

Krystal shakes her head. Gary gets out his phone and starts dialling but she stops him.

KRYSTAL   It's a waste of time. They never come.

GARY   At least let me phone an ambulance then? You need to be seen by a doctor.

KRYSTAL   Could you take me?

GARY   Of course.

Gary tries to help Krystal up, but she resists.

KRYSTAL   Just give me a minute.

He looks around at the carnage before him.

You know you didn't need to book to see me. I wanted to help you. I wanted to help you be who you wanted to be. I thought I helped. I wanted to help. And then you just stopped coming. I thought you might have messaged or something. I thought about you. About what you might have done next, whether you'd have contacted Rachel or suddenly gone of a mad sex spree or something. I tried looking for you online. I even looked for you on the council's staff page, but you never seemed to show up. I just happened to be looking at the local news bit one day when suddenly I saw a picture of that Mayor wanker opening some park or something when I spotted a familiar face. I looked at all the names credit at the bottom, but it didn't say Gary. Justin. Secretary to the honourable what's his face Justin Barker-Smith!

I know I'm not exactly in the business for customers to tell the truth to me and I don't mind that. People come, people fuck, people go. I don't get attached. I don't get emotional. But you were my friend! I've spent more hours talking with you than any other person I have ever met! You know me. You know me more than anyone else. And I thought I knew you.

Silence.

GARY Krystal...

KRYSTAL It's fine. Don't worry about it.

Krystal tries to get herself up off the caravan step.

JUSTIN I'm Justin Barker-Smith. I live in a two up, two down terraced house, barely big enough to swing a cat. I live with my hamster, Gerald. I'm the secretary to the town mayor which basically means I open his mail and tell him where he's meant to be each day. I suffer big time with panic attacks and don't do well when put on the spot. I don't have many friends but those I do have I would move the

Earth for. And I would be honoured if you would let me call you a friend.

Krystal looks on the verge of tears.

KRYSTAL   I think I'd like that.

Justin smiles.

JUSTIN   Let's get you looked at first.

Krystal nods. Justin helps her up and they both leave.

Justin re-appears and starts tidying everything up.

The caravan is almost back to normal now. There is tape on some of the walls and windows where things were damaged, but all furniture is back how it was. Justin walks off...

...and returns helping Krystal. She looks around at her belongings.

KRYSTAL   You didn't have to tidy up.

JUSTIN   It's fine. I didn't mind.

KRYSTAL   Thank you.

JUSTIN   Do you want a drink. I'm afraid I haven't got any fresh stuff in for you 'cause, well, I didn't really know what you normally had in. There's still some tea and things in the cupboard though.

KRYSTAL   I'm fine. Thank you.

Krystal looks around the space.

JUSTIN I've been thinking.

Krystal doesn't really respond. She is distracted by everything around her.

Maybe you should stay with me for a bit.

KRYSTAL What?

JUSTIN Yeah.

KRYSTAL I couldn't do that. That's just ridiculous.

JUSTIN Is it?

Beat.

You can't stay here. Not now at least. You can barely walk, from the bed to the toilet. The door doesn't even close properly. And what if he comes back?

KRYSTAL He won't come back. They never do after this.

JUSTIN Well, either way. You're not exactly in a fit state to work just yet. Not face to face at least. Why couldn't you stay with me?

KRYSTAL You don't like change. You said it yourself.

JUSTIN It's worth it.

KRYSTAL I don't know.

JUSTIN   You're my friend.

Beat.

You helped *me* once.

Krystal just nods her head agreeingly.

Transition. During this transition Justin packs up some of Krystal's things into a suitcase.

KRYSTAL   So I think this is where I showed you at the start. Just the two of us, alone in my caravan, my home. I want to thank you all for listening to my story tonight. For helping me tell it. For letting me share my life with you and for sharing yours with me in return. I can't say there's a simple message or clear moral to this story, but it's mine and I own that.

JUSTIN   It's time for us to go.

KRYSTAL   Ok, just give me a minute.

Transition.

Justin and Krystal are standing in the caravan. They are looking at each other, both feel a mix of emotions; panic, excitement, nervousness, and fear. They stand in silence for a moment, just staring at each other. She has two suitcases beside her.

JUSTIN   Are you sure you want to do this?

KRYSTAL   Every damn thing you do in this life, you have to pay for.

Blackout.

A CARAVAN NAMED DESIRE
(THE KASTOR SCRIPT)

A Caravan Named Desire – The Kastor Script has only ever been workshopped by Helen and Alexander Millington with support from public funding by the National Lottery through Arts Council England. The cast was as follows:

Kastor   Alexander Millington

Gabi   Helen Millington

Director   Helen Millington

CHARACTERS

KASTOR
early to mid 30s.

GABI
older than Kastor.

Lines written in bold are directly addressed to the audience. Wherever possible, the audience should be invited to join the conversations between Alexander and Helen.

The stage is filled with an old caravan with one side removed so that the audience can see the action within. It has been cared for over the years, but some wear and tear is unavoidable. It looks like it hasn't been moved for a long time. When scenes are exterior to the caravan, they can be performed either in front of the removed wall or the caravan can be rotated. Outside the caravan there are some old camping chairs and a table. Unless otherwise stated, all scenes are at night and the lighting should demonstrate this. The interior of the caravan is lit with old lamps, fairy lights, and one single, bare hanging bulb in the centre of the main living space. The interior of the caravan is surprisingly clean and tidy, though very dated, possibly 80s or early 90s decor. It is cramped, and most of the furniture needs some form of unfolding or setting up.

Gabi and Kastor are standing in the caravan. They are looking at each other, both feel a mix of emotions; panic, excitement, nervousness, and fear. They stand in silence for a moment, just staring at each other.

GABI   Are you ready?

The lights blow and they are left in darkness. Gabi disappears in the darkness. Kastor comes forward to the audience.

Transition.

Kastor is tidying up items inside the caravan. Some items he may collect from off stage to put in position. He looks at the audience.

KASTOR   Don't mind me. I'm just getting everything set up.

He carries on moving some things around before stopping and staring into the audience.

I know what you're thinking. Shit! Where's the fucking fourth wall. This twat could have me doing some kind of interactive shit. Maybe I will. But not much. You see, that's the point of this really. In a way. Trust. You see most of the time you trust the performer not to talk to you, touch you, invite you into the space. This is the space by the way. It's a caravan. Well, it's a set made up to look like a caravan. Again, this is where I need you to trust me, trust the set. Forget that we're currently in the [name

of space] and believe we're actually outside, and occasionally inside, a caravan. Now, a lot of what you are going to see tonight is true, by which I mean a representation of the truth, of events that have happened. A dramatisation of real life, real events. Inspired by, based upon. Not exactly a fallacy, more of an interpretation. What I'm trying to say is that this is all true, completely true... except for the bits that aren't. I swear. Now, before I go any further do we have any questions? Have I said anything that's been unclear at all?

If questions are asked then Kastor must do his best to answer these questions.

Ok, now that all the formalities are dealt with, onto the story itself. Now, my name is Kastor, that's Kastor with a K by the way, not a C. And this is my home. I'm... well, I'm many things, depending on who you talk to. If you're talking to my mum for instance, I'm an entrepreneur and manager of a little online shop which sells second hand stuff. If you're talking to people online, I'm a model and independent film star. If you ask HMRC, then I'm an entertainer. But, if you want to ask me directly... well, you'll just have to wait and make up your own minds. But what I do isn't the main point of

> this story, it's more about Gabi. Now Gabi...
> you know what, this isn't a solo show. I'll just
> let it get started and come back to you in a bit.

Transition.

Kastor climbs back into the caravan and begins hunting for a light bulb. Once he has found one, he replaces the bulb that blew, and the lights come back on completely red. There is a knocking at the door.

> Just a minute!

Kastor then turns on a lamp with a clear bulb to balance the light. Gabi is waiting at the caravan door wearing a button through blouse and skirt, as if she has just come from work. Everything is a little bit creased, and clearly a little bit old. She knocks again.

> Just a sec!

Kastor turns on some fairy lights that trail around the caravan. He has to click the button a few times to work through the pre-sets before he settles on one. He checks himself in a small mirror before going to the door and opening it.

> Sorry about that, bloody fuse went again. It's always doing it. Oh. Sorry, I wasn't expecting... I'll just be a sec. Well, come in.

Gabi enters and is directed across to the other end of the caravan. Kastor goes to the bathroom, the only place not entirely visible to Gabi, but is to the audience. Kastor pulls out a small money bag from within the toilet cistern. It contains some notes. He pulls out a few notes and returns the remaining money to where he found it. He returns to Gabi.

> You must be Tony's new bird. I wasn't expecting him to send you alone, he should have at least come with you. I told Tony it was going to be a bit short this month 'cause the internet kept cutting out, so my loss of income is due to him. We've talked about it though and he said it's fine so no need to bother him with the details. Well here, aren't you going to take it?

Kastor thrusts the money towards Gabi. Gabi, uncertain of what to do, slowly reaches for the money. Before she touches it, Kastor pulls it back.

	Hang on. What's your name again?
GABI	Gabi. My name's Gabi.
KASTOR	You're not Uncle Tony's new missus.
GABI	Erm… no. I don't know your Uncle Tony. I sent you a message last week. We'd arranged to meet.
KASTOR	Thursday. We said we'd meet on Thursday. It's not fucking Thursday today is it?
GABI	No. No, it's Wednesday today.
KASTOR	We did say Thursday, didn't we?

GABI   Oh yes, we did. I'm early.

KASTOR   By twenty-four-fucking-hours. You made me think I'd lost a fucking day or something, Jesus Christ! You don't do that to somebody! Do you have any idea what shit you might have caused by making me think I'd lost a day. I might have plans, very specific plans, you know, which I have to do on a Thursday and now all of a sudden I've lost my Thursday and forgotten to do everything!

GABI   It's not Thursday though, it's Wednesday.

KASTOR   I know that now! I knew that five minutes ago. But the time between five minutes ago and now I thought it was fucking Thursday! Fuck me I need a sit down.

GABI   I'm sorry.

Kastor tucks the cash into his pocket.

KASTOR   I should think so too. Why are you here anyway?

GABI   I'm sorry. I just, I wanted to make sure I knew the way when I came tomorrow. Make sure I didn't get lost. Or that it wasn't some fake address or something. So, I put the address you gave me into my phone and, as you said, it directed me to this site, and then

	I saw the caravan and thought, well, whilst I'm here I should probably just knock and check it's the right one. I didn't want to come tomorrow and find I was at the wrong door.
KASTOR	Right, well… you've found me. Congratulations.
GABI	Thank you.

Beat.

KASTOR	Was there anything else?
GABI	Oh, sorry, no. I just wanted to make sure I knew the way. I should be going actually. Nice to have met you.
KASTOR	Wait, wait, wait. Since you're here, do you want to…?
GABI	Oh, no, no thank you. I've got to get back. But I'll definitely be back tomorrow. I'll see myself out.

Gabi goes to exit the caravan and closes the door behind her.

KASTOR	Alright. Well, see ya.

Transition.

So, that was Gabi. A close encounter of… the weird kind. I can't say I held out much hope as to whether she would even turn up the next

night. She looked like a deer in the headlights just standing in the fucking door. I couldn't tell if she was religious weird or just, you know, kinky weird. Was she gonna turn up tomorrow to try and convert me to Mormonism, or come with a full on leather gimp suit underneath her top? I mean who turns up twenty-four hours early for an appointment just to check they know the way. And who knocks on the door! She did come back the next day. Though I've got to say, she still didn't fill me with much confidence. I'm glad I took the initial money upfront.

Transition.

Kastor is laid on the sofa bed going through some paperwork. He keeps looking at the clock hanging on the wall. He then taps on his phone to check the time is correct. Gabi is outside the caravan, sitting in one of the camping chairs. Eventually, Kastor goes to the caravan door and opens it. He looks about until he spots Gabi sitting in the chair and is startled.

KASTOR   Jesus Christ! What the fuck are you doing sat there?!

Gabi is startled by his response.

GABI   Sorry. I came to your door, but I was a little early and wasn't sure if you might be busy, so

	I thought I'd just wait out here for a minute. I guess I must have lost track of time.
KASTOR	You were meant to have been here at seven.
GABI	I know.
KASTOR	It's nine!
GABI	I know. I lost track of time.
KASTOR	Fuck me.
GABI	Should I come back another time?
KASTOR	No. No, it's fine. I'm charging you as if you were here from seven though.
GABI	Ok.
KASTOR	(*to himself.*) Two fucking hours.
GABI	What do we do now then?
KASTOR	Do you wanna come in?
GABI	Can do.
KASTOR	Unless you wanna do it out here?
GABI	Would you like to?
KASTOR	I was kidding. It's fucking freezing out here.
GABI	Sorry.

Beat.

	It's a lovely night.
KASTOR	Yeah?

Kastor looks up at the sky.

	Yeah, I suppose it is.
GABI	The moon's so bright.
KASTOR	I prefer new moons myself.
GABI	Yeah?
KASTOR	You can see the stars better then. The moonlight blocks out a lot of the stars.
GABI	At New Moon you're also meant to bow and turn over any of your silver for good luck… or a new love.
KASTOR	Yeah?

Beat

	Well, come in then. I'm letting all the cold in here!

Gabi gets up out of the chair and enters the caravan. Kastor shuts the door behind them.

	I can see you're going to be trouble.
GABI	I don't mean to be.

KASTOR	I'm sure. You just go from twenty-four hours early to two hours late. What would you have done if someone else turned up?
GABI	Erm… I don't really know. Left, I suppose.
KASTOR	Well, you're lucky I'm quiet at the moment. And in a good mood. Look, why don't you take a seat. Do you want a drink?
GABI	Oh, nothing for me, thank you.
KASTOR	Then take a seat while I make myself a drink.

Kastor gets a bottle of squash and water out of a cupboard along with a glass and pours himself a drink. He takes a swig then tops up the glass. Gabi is looking for somewhere to sit down. She goes to sit on the sofa bed but doesn't want to disturb the papers that are there. She starts to move some of them when Kastor turns around and sees her.

Don't fucking move those!

Kastor rushes across the caravan and grabs at the papers, trying to put them back how they were.

GABI	I'm sorry. I was just trying to find somewhere to sit.
KASTOR	So you start fucking with my tax returns?
GABI	Tax returns?

Kastor takes Gabi by the shoulders and places her on the sofa bed where he has made a small space beside the papers.

KASTOR	Yeah, my fucking tax return. I'm not exactly PAYE doing this, am I? Now, just sit there, and don't move, alright.
GABI	Sorry.
KASTOR	And stop apologising.

Gabi goes to apologise again but stops herself.

Now, before we go any further, have you got money?

Gabi reaches into her handbag and pulls out her purse.

GABI	Did it not come through? I used the link you sent me when I booked.
KASTOR	That was for one hour. I'm charging you for three now, remember.
GABI	Oh, yes. Sorry. How much? I've only got…
KASTOR	Hang on, let me work it out. Now, you've wasted two hours already, so that's going to be £160. £80 an hour whether we do anything or not, no negotiation. Now, what is it you actually want? You didn't go into much detail before.
GABI	Well…

KASTOR   I'm open to most things but I do have my limits.

GABI   All I really want is…erm…well…

KASTOR   Come on, spit it out.

GABI   Can we just talk?

KASTOR   Talk?

GABI   Yeah.

KASTOR   I take it back, I will take the money first.

GABI   I'm not saying I definitely don't want to do anything, I'm just not sure that I will.

KASTOR   So what *might* you want to do? Want me to finger you, go down on you, fuck you? If so, front or back? Want a facial, fisting, pegging? Do you want to suck my dick, rim me, be rimmed…?

GABI   I don't know. I probably won't want to try anything. At least not tonight. I don't even know half of the stuff you said then. Maybe if we hit it off we could arrange a second night. I don't really know. I've never done this before. I'm sorry. Maybe I should just go now.

Gabi gets up to leave but Kastor stands in her way.

KASTOR   £240 and you just wanna talk? Stay for the hour, and we'll talk. That's all that's covered, mind. Anything else happens, that's extra.

GABI   Ok.

Gabi gets out her purse again and takes out some cash.

                I've only got £50 with me.

KASTOR   I take card.

Gabi takes a card out of her purse. Kastor picks up his card machine from amongst the paperwork on the bed. There's an awkward silence while Kastor waits for the machine to load. He offers the device to Gabi.

                Tap it.

Gabi does so. The transaction goes through. Kastor returns the machine back with the paperwork.

                Right. So, what do you wanna talk about?

Transition.

I hope this isn't breaking up the action too much for you. I don't mean it to, it's just there isn't much point in you watching the next hour when it's just talking. There wasn't even much of that actually, to be fair. There were probably more pauses and silences than talking. And there's no point me making you watch an hour

of just pauses and silences. I mean you might as well go and watch a Beckett or a Pinter if you're just gonna watch a silent stage.

Anyway, you didn't miss much. I couldn't even tell you if what we talked about was the truth or not. In fact, the only thing she told me, which I can be fairly certain is true, was that she was a virgin! Now, I'm not here to judge. People have all sorts of reasons for not wanting to do it. Saving it for marriage. Just not met the right person yet. Not had the opportunity. But Gabi, well, who knows! I like to treat a person's virginity, or at least their first sexual experiences, like a game of Cluedo. Me for example: Ms Morris, behind the cinema, with my fingers. One of my old teachers, never did get her first name. Chrissy Sinclair, inside my Dad's shed, from behind. I still come over all funny when I get the smell of creosote. Mr Wallace, on the back seat of his Toyota Corolla, wearing his wife's knickers. Him, not me. That was my first bloke. I make it sound as if I've never had it 'normal'. A loving girlfriend, on the bed, missionary. It's just not as exciting to talk about really, is it?

Now, as I said, Gabi and I didn't do anything on that first visit. We didn't do anything for

her first three visits! The talking got a little better. But it was still just small talk. It was on her fourth visit however when things started to get a little bit more interesting.

Transition.

Gabi is pacing around outside the caravan. Kastor is standing at the door as before, trying to convince her to come in.

KASTOR   Look, the longer you stay out here the colder my caravan's going to get and then we'll both be complaining. Now, why don't you just get in here and tell me what's shit in your knickers today?

GABI   Nothing's shit in my knickers!

                Do you like me?

KASTOR   Do I what?

GABI   Do you like me?

KASTOR   To be honest you're freaking me out a little bit.

GABI   I know you don't *like me* like me, that's not what I'm asking. What I'm asking is do you... do you think I'm an alright person.

KASTOR   I've only met you a handful of times and even then you barely speak, so I can't really say. I doubt you're a complete twat if that's what you mean?

GABI Ok.

KASTOR I'm not saying I've completely ruled it out, mind. You might still pull a knife on me yet.

GABI I think I like you.

KASTOR Right.

GABI Not, like that. I could never like you like that.

KASTOR Good to know.

GABI I don't mean it like that. I just mean, I like you as a person, an acquaintance, sort of.

Beat.

I don't think you're a complete twat either.

They both smile. This is the first time they both seem relaxed.

KASTOR Look, why don't you come in, I'll make us both a drink and we can have a chat again.

Kastor turns to get some cans of drink out of his cupboard. Gabi just stands and stares at him.

GABI I want to do more than just talk tonight.

Kastor turns to look at her.

If that's ok.

KASTOR	Erm. Sure. Yeah. What did you have in mind?
GABI	I don't know.
KASTOR	Right.
GABI	I just... I want to try something new.

Pause.

KASTOR	Alright. I'll get those drinks.

Kastor gets out some cups to pour the drinks into but changes his mind.

GABI	I don't drink.
KASTOR	I get the impression you're going to need something. It's only coke anyway.
GABI	Can I just have a water?
KASTOR	Alright.

Kastor gets out a bottle of water and passes it to Gabi. Gabi just watches him, not thinking to take the bottle from him. Kastor just places it on the side. She takes a step towards him as if about to do something but is unsure what. She takes a step back, sees the water and takes a mouthful.

GABI	Do you kiss and cuddle and stuff?
KASTOR	Kiss and cuddle?

GABI   I know some…

KASTOR   Some?

GABI   What do you like to be called?

KASTOR   Kastor.

GABI   I mean…

KASTOR   I know what you mean. I'm Kastor.

GABI   Well, I just know some… Kastors that don't do kissing and cuddles.

KASTOR   Know many Kastors do you?

GABI   Well, no. I mean I've heard, or rather seen on TV, that some don't like to do all that stuff.

KASTOR   Do you like to kiss and cuddle?

Gabi doesn't know how to respond for a second before eventually nodding.

            Then we can kiss and cuddle.

GABI   Ok. Ok.

Kastor moves close to Gabi. Gabi stands still but begins to prepare herself for a kiss.

Transition.

KASTOR   Her hands were all over me. Her fingers running through my hair, pulling my face into

hers. I felt her fingers slowly run down my back before grabbing my arse. Our bodies rubbing together, her tits pressed up against me. I could feel her hands making their way round to my belt! She whipped it off me, ripped open her top and dropped to her knees...! I'm just kidding you. Can you seriously imagine her...? We just kissed. But, you know what, she wasn't too bad. Good even. Eventually. A little awkward and tentative to start with but she began to get into it after a while. It was a bit like being back in school.

Who here remembers the name of their first kiss by the way, you don't need to call it out, just a show of hands. Everyone remembers their first. Ok, a little trickier now. Who remembers *how many* people they've kissed, the actual number, not a round abouts? And their names? So, we're not really all that different are we. Some of us, anyway. Selena was my first. Selena McDermott. This geeky little blonde girl who fancied me in primary school. A load of us were playing kiss chase and the other girls pressured her into playing. She had me pinned in the corner. She clearly didn't know what to do so *I* kissed *her*. She went bright red and ran off, apparently she went and threw her guts up in the toilet or

something. But that's just school gossip, who really knows.

Transition.

Gabi is sitting on the sofa bed. Kastor is in the kitchen area making himself another drink.

KASTOR   So be honest, was that your first kiss?

Gabi seems to be just staring off into the middle distance, holding her bottle of water.

GABI   No!

KASTOR   No?

GABI   Year 5. Dale French, St Mary's Primary School. A load of the other girls were playing kiss chase and pressured me in to playing. I had him pinned in the corner. I think he could tell I didn't know what to do so he kissed me. I went bright red and ran and hid in the toilets. I thought I was going to be sick.

KASTOR   Did he kiss you as his name suggests?

GABI   Pardon?

KASTOR   French?

GABI   We were only nine!

KASTOR   You done with that bottle?

Beat.

GABI   I lied to you, Kastor.

Transition.

KASTOR   **Lies aren't anything new. If anything, it's expected. It's unusual if they don't lie to be honest. I mean let's face it, if you were given the chance to be anyone you want to be, which is basically what's on offer here isn't it? The chance to be whoever you want to be. Make your dreams come true. Even if it's just for an hour or two. Why would you be yourself? But I wasn't expecting her to say what she told me next.**

Transition.

GABI   I'm married.

KASTOR   Oh.

GABI   Well, not anymore.

KASTOR   Ok.

GABI   Divorced. Soon to be anyway.

KASTOR   I'm sorry?

GABI   Papers are all filed now. I just thought you should know.

KASTOR	Hey, I'm not here to judge. Plenty of the people come to see me after a relationship. Hell, most people see me when they're still in a relationship. That's nothing new.
GABI	It's just…
KASTOR	Hang on, does this mean you're not a virgin?
GABI	Well, not exactly.
KASTOR	Well you either are or you aren't. Either way, it doesn't really bother me. You can say what you want, it's you paying for the time.
GABI	It's just, I have had sex… I've just never… I don't think I've actually… finished.
KASTOR	What do you mean?
GABI	I'm… well, I struggle.
KASTOR	Right.
GABI	Or at least, I've never not struggled.

Beat.

You see, I've… not been with many men. I mean I had boyfriends and things before I got married but they were just little school romances, so we never really did anything. Well, except this one time where Callum Jordan invited me to go to the cinema with him and before the we went in, he took me round the back and started to touch me, which I wanted him to do, but I began to feel guilty and left and never spoke to him again.

Beat.

You see Richard and I, that's my husband, was my husband, we'd only done it once before we got married and I was so nervous I never really relaxed into it. I thought it'd get better as we got used to each other, but it never did so whenever we had sex, no matter how much I wanted to enjoy it I just... never did.

KASTOR   Ok. So when you say you're a virgin, you mean... what?

GABI   I've never... actually... finished with anyone. Even if it's started off well and I wanted to get into it I just never managed to...

KASTOR   Cum?

GABI   No.

KASTOR   But you do when you wank right? You do wank don't you? Masturbate? Flick the bean? Schlicking? Rolling the pill? Paddling the pink canoe? Dialling the old rotary phone? Visit the downstairs DJ?

GABI   Erm... Do you mind if I just take a minute? I'm just getting a bit... sorry.

Gabi rushes outside of the caravan to try and catch her breath. Kastor stands at the door of the caravan and watches her.

KASTOR   You alright?

GABI   No. I get like this. I don't really know why I'm here. I don't know what's wrong with me.

KASTOR   It's alright, just take a breath. Nothing's wrong with you. You want another water or something?

GABI   No, I'll be alright. I just need...

Gabi sits down on one of the camping chairs again. She looks up at the sky.

                You're right. You can see more stars without the moon.

Kastor steps out of the caravan and looks up.

KASTOR   Beautiful, isn't it? If you look over there you'll see the Big Dipper.

GABI   I can never see those things.

KASTOR   The constellations? Look, see that trapezium sort of shape there?

GABI   The what?

KASTOR   The sort of square shape, over there?

GABI   I think so?

KASTOR   And those three stars going up at an angle? That's the Big Dipper. People always say it looks like a saucepan or something, I dunno. And those three there, that's Orion's Belt. That was the first constellation I learnt. And that little cluster of stars there is the Seven Sisters.

Gabi starts to relax.

GABI   How do you know all of these?

KASTOR   I dunno. I just do. I'm not just some bimbo, alright. I do know things.

GABI   Sorry.

KASTOR   It's alright.

Beat.

GABI   I just want to know what it's like.

KASTOR   What it's like to be a constellation?

GABI   To be with someone... and enjoy it.

KASTOR   Oh. We can work on that. Why now though? You've got to be what, 40, 45?

GABI   I'm 39!

KASTOR	Sorry. But surely you've come at least close to it, once? Did you never discuss it with your husband?
	You don't have to tell me. It might just help me to work out what...
GABI	He cheated.
KASTOR	Oh.
GABI	I came home one day, and he was just sat on the sofa crying. I thought something awful had happened. He said being with me was making him feel unattractive and making him think that I wasn't happy being with him. I told him this wasn't the case but... I tried to suggest that we went to counselling or maybe we should try spicing things up a bit in the bedroom.
	Six years we were together. Married for four. At the start we tried a few things to try and find something that worked for me. We did it in different positions and different rooms of the house. We even tried outside once. He took me out to the shed, but the smell of the creosote just kept distracting me.

Transition.

KASTOR	**This went on for some time so I'm just going to cut to the end bit. It's the only key bit really.**

Transition.

GABI	He said that he'd slept with someone from work. He didn't even say he was sorry or that it was a mistake or that he regretted it. He just came out with it and said it. Next thing I know he's walked out the door and I'm the one crying on the sofa.

Sorry. I did consider just hooking up with some stranger on a night out but, well, I've never been one of these one-night stand kinds of people.

Kastor looks at his watch. Time is nearly up.

There were the odd times where things seemed to happen organically and that was nice, but then I'd start to get self-conscious about it and get worried. As soon as I start to think about it, it just… I'm just not in the mood.

Kastor looks at his watch again. He begins to try and move things along. Time is up.

KASTOR	You're over thinking all of this. Just get a plan together and go for it!

GABI I can't do a plan. If I have a plan and something goes wrong then I'll just worry about that.

KASTOR Spontaneity then.

GABI I hear you can get these things off the internet now, like a lady masturbator, they're supposed to be good, I could get one of those for next time.

KASTOR Toys are certainly one way to do it, but I'm afraid…

GABI Though I've never really been all good at that either. How can you not even be good at doing it to yourself?

KASTOR That's a good question, have a think about it.

Gabi is not taking the hint to leave.

GABI Could we just try a kiss again. See if I feel anything.

KASTOR Maybe next time.

GABI Next time?

KASTOR I've got another…

GABI Another what?

KASTOR Your times up. I've got another appointment.

GABI	Oh. Sorry. I didn't realise. You should have said.
KASTOR	Next time. We'll see what's gonna be best for you.
GABI	Ok. I'll book it when I get home. Same time work for you?
KASTOR	Yes. Yeah, that's fine. Please, though, if you wouldn't mind. I've really got to get ready.
GABI	Oh. Yes. Of course. Sorry.

Gabi makes her way off. She looks back at Kastor.

> You can just tell me to shut up by the way. I don't normally talk all that much with new people. I guess you make me feel at ease. Comfortable.

Kastor smiles.

KASTOR   See you next time.

Gabi exits. As soon as she's out of sight, Kastor, starts tidying up the caravan: making the bed, putting away the mugs. He pulls out a cooler of canned drinks. The cooler contains a variety of soft drinks and water. Kastor places the cooler between the two camping chairs at the front.

Transition.

I do hate a rush. I'm self-employed for a reason. I can stick to my own schedule, I don't have to answer to anyone, so as soon as someone starts fucking with my plans I quickly start to lose my shit. Time is money, as they say.

Show of hands, who uses an alarm to wake you up? Do you snooze it though? Alarm set for six but don't get up till seven sort of thing? I can't do that. I set the alarm - I get up with that alarm. I have to. You do if you're your own boss. I have a very strict routine otherwise I never get anything done.

Evenings and nights vary from day to day of course. I've got my regulars that I go to see. Clare's nice. Tuesday evenings, seven-thirty. She's a young widow, fifties I think. She just gets lonely, and I think Tuesday used to be her regular with her husband. Then there's the three Ms: Martine, Megan and Matthew. They're all Friday night. One after the other. Matthew I have to come back here for though. Women tend to like you to go to them, but the guys don't really want to do it in their own places. Probably because they've got a wife and kid waiting for them at home. Then there are semi-regulars. Once a fortnight or once a

> month-ers. Occasionals and of course one-offs and new clients. I usually try and have Sundays and Mondays off for general admin but depending on how the month's going I might take the odd bit of work here and there. Women tend to plan ahead but men can be more in the moment so if I get a last minute ping through I might go for it. It is a full-time job doing this.

Kastor opens the cooler and makes it clear to the audience what is inside.

> Anyone want a drink by the way? It's just soft drinks.

Kastor hands some drinks out to people, one of whom he invites to sit in one of the camping chairs.

> Is that comfortable enough for you? Are you alright there? I'm just going to quickly grab something.

Kastor goes back inside the caravan, leaving the audience member in the chair.

> I'll just be a second!

Transition.

Gabi enters but freezes as soon as she sees the person in the camping chair. Gabi looks at her watch then back at the other person. Gabi walks off for a moment before returning, still confused. She offers a hand to the other person to shake.

GABI　　　　　Hello. Gabi.

The audience member may or may not reply.

> I thought I must have been early, but only a couple of minutes. Is he still…? Do you mind if I just sit and wait with you? I don't want to intrude if…

Gabi sits in the second camping chair.

> Is it just you here? There isn't someone else in with him I mean or have you just…?

The audience member may or may not reply.

> Sorry. I shouldn't ask. None of my business. Sorry.

Beat.

> Lovely night. Not too cold. Or too warm. Just right. What is it you're drinking?

Kastor walks out of the caravan and sees the two clients together.

KASTOR　　　Sorry about that, I just had to find a card with the correct details on. Oh…erm. Sorry, you're early?

GABI　　　　　Only by a couple of minutes.

KASTOR   (*To audience member.*) I'm sorry about this. Here, drop me a message and we'll arrange another appointment.

Kastor ushers off the audience member. Gabi tries to shake hands with them again before they go. Gabi remains in her camping chair.

GABI   They seemed nice. Chatty.

Kastor sits in the other camping chair and chooses a drink from the cooler.

                New regular?

KASTOR   Why do you still come here, Gabi?

GABI   What do you mean? You know why.

KASTOR   It's been three months.

Beat.

                Aside from the occasional kissing session we haven't even tried anything. I'm not trying to turn you away or anything, I'd just like to know where this is going? Which seems like an odd question under the circumstances I know, but, c'mon. Don't we know each other enough yet for you try a bit more?

GABI   I… I don't know. You're kind of putting me on the spot. I don't know.

KASTOR   Well, let's find out shall we.

Kastor moves to kiss Gabi passionately, taking her by surprise. Kastor stops and slowly pulls his face away from Gabi's.

KASTOR　　　　How was that?

Gabi nods her head, a little embarrassed.

GABI　　　　　I can't promise it'll last though.

KASTOR　　　　Then let's not waste our chance.

Kastor repositions himself so that his hand is down Gabi's trousers. He begins to work.

KASTOR　　　　How's that?

Gabi nods, her breathing now becoming erratic.

　　　　　　　　That's it. C'mon. Come on.

Gabi's face starts to look different, as if she is concentrating a lot.

　　　　　　　　Think of something. Think of something that turns you on. Think of something that gets you off. Richard. Another ex. Your celebrity crush. C'mon!

GABI　　　　　I don't know.

KASTOR　　　　Picture the perfect guy. He looks amazing. He's calling you to him. He's… [*Kastor begins describing a member of the audience: their clothes, their hair, their eyes, etc. in as much detail as possible.*] He looks at you, dead in the eye and tells you he wants you.

GABI Yes?

KASTOR You can feel yourself getting wet. You want him.

Gabi's face continues to look uncomfortably focused before she seems to give up.

GABI It's gone. I'm sorry.

Kastor carries on for a second.

KASTOR Stay with me. C'mon, tell me what you want him to do to you.

Gabi takes a gentle hold of Kastor's wrist, stopping him.

GABI It's too late.

Kastor retrieves his hand and, deflated, sits in the other camping chair.

Sorry.

KASTOR What are you apologising for? I'm the one that didn't get you there.

GABI There was just too much pressure.

KASTOR There's no pressure. I was trying to be more spontaneous – even less pressure really.

GABI	Not for me. I've had no chance to prepare myself for what might happen. Then, as it happens, I was wondering how far it's gonna go. Then I worry that maybe it will go further but I'll lose it. Then once I start to think I'm gonna lose it that's all I can think about and then…
KASTOR	You lose it.
GABI	Yeah.

Transition.

KASTOR You know what, I've got to say I was pleasantly surprised by her honesty. I mean let's face it, how many women would admit they struggle to enjoy sex? I bet most of you would just fake it. Men wouldn't say the same, whether they struggle to get it up or not. Men don't like that question, or rather, they don't like the truth behind the answer to that question. But Gabi was really quite open. Maybe that's just women though. Men hide from the truth whereas women try and change it.

You see the problem with Gabi was this block she had if she didn't know you well enough. We were coming up to six months now. What more did she need to know? How much longer

> was it gonna take to get to know me. I asked her.

Transition.

> How much longer is it gonna take to get to know me?

Transition.

> She couldn't tell me. I mean you don't know, do you?
>
> I made a suggestion for her next visit. That we just talk. Back to step one, but this time with a specific topic of conversation. Has anyone here heard of the 36 questions?

If someone says yes, then Kastor can engage them in conversation to see how much they know.

> Well, there are these 36 questions right which, if discussed with a partner, are meant to create a really close and intimate bond between you. Nothing too fancy, it's just meant to be an exercise to get to know someone essentially. *The Experimental Generation of Interpersonal Closeness: A Procedure and Some Preliminary Findings* accredited to Dr Arthur Aron and his colleagues. For those non academics in here, it was also in Cosmo last year, snappily titled 36

Questions to Fall in Love, and has featured in a dozen other magazines before that.

Transition.

The two camping chairs are now positioned to be facing one another. Gabi is sitting on one, holding a piece of paper. Kastor is getting himself a drink from inside the caravan before coming out to join Gabi, sitting in the opposite chair.

GABI So what do we do?

KASTOR Just work our way through the questions. You ask a question and we both answer, then I ask a question which we both answer, until we've both answered all 36. We've got to be honest though.

GABI And then what?

KASTOR Well, then you know me. And I know you. It might just sort our little problem out and we can try some stuff.

GABI So who goes first?

KASTOR You go.

GABI Ok. Set 1 slip 1. Actually, before we start, there is one thing I'd like to ask.

KASTOR Yeah?

GABI Kastor? Is that really your name?

KASTOR   It's how I like to be referred to.

GABI   But were you born Kastor?

KASTOR   Are any of us born...

GABI   Never mind. I just wondered that was all. It doesn't matter. Set 1, slip 1...

KASTOR   Vincent.

GABI   What?

KASTOR   My mum called me Vincent. After Vincent van Gogh.

GABI   As in the *Starry Night* guy?

KASTOR   Yes.

GABI   Vincent.

KASTOR   Don't.

GABI   I think it suits...

KASTOR   No it doesn't. And it's not the name I chose at birth, and it's not the name I choose now, alright?

GABI   Ok.

KASTOR   Start us off then.

GABI   Ok. Slip 1: Given the choice of anyone in the world, whom would you want as a dinner guest?

Pause.

KASTOR   Now, you answer first since you asked the question, then I'll answer.

GABI   Oh, erm… Is it living or dead?

KASTOR   Try not to over think it. Just go for, first name in your head.

GABI   My grandmother. Before she got ill. She's dead now, but I'd love to have one more meal with her. Hear her stories and her laugh.

KASTOR   That's nice.

GABI   Thank you. You?

KASTOR   Phaedo of Elis.

GABI   Who?!

KASTOR   He's an ancient Greek Philosopher. He was enslaved as a prostitute before Socrates and his mates bought him his freedom.

GABI   Why'd you wanna meet him?

KASTOR   I just think it'd be cool to know what it was like back then and how it felt to become free.

GABI   Fair enough.

KASTOR   Slip 2: Would you like to be famous? If so, in what way?

Transition.

KASTOR   You get the gist. I'm not going to show you all 36 questions, but I just wanted to share a few of the key ones with you.

Transition.

Time moves forward.

            Slip 8: Name three things you and your partner appear to have in common.

GABI   Shit.

KASTOR   It's not that hard.

Time moves forward.

GABI   Slip 13: If a crystal ball could tell you the truth about yourself, your life, the future, or anything else, what would you want to know? Will I ever enjoy sex with someone?

Time moves forward.

KASTOR   That was the first time I properly saw a planet. We looked round the whole sky and he taught me… that's when I learnt the constellations. At the end of the night, when he dropped me back off at home, he gave me the telescope. Said it was mine. He said he was moving away and wouldn't have any space for it and knew it would go to good use with me.

Time moves forward.

Slip 20: What does friendship mean to you? Trust.

GABI   That all?

KASTOR   If you have trust, what more do you need?

GABI   I guess so. I mean I still want trust, but I also need a sense of humour, good conversation, likes going out for meals or coming and going round each other's houses to chill.

KASTOR   You make it sound like you want a date with everyone you know.

Time moves forward.

KASTOR   Complete this sentence: "I wish I had someone with whom I could share…" my life, I guess.

GABI   Yeah?

KASTOR	Yeah. I know this career doesn't scream boyfriend material, but I'd like to meet someone someday who gets me and wants to be with me. I could still do the online stuff. I just need to find someone who gets me and will let me be who I want to be.
GABI	I get you.
KASTOR	Thanks. How about you?
GABI	I wish I had someone with whom I could share… everything.
KASTOR	Everything?
GABI	Yeah, everything. All my secrets and worries and fears and dreams and…well, everything.

Time moves forward.

> If you were to die this evening with no opportunity to communicate with anyone, what would you most regret not having told someone? Why haven't you told them yet?

Beat.

KASTOR	You ok?

Time moves forward.

> Slip 36: Share a personal problem and ask your partner's advice on how they might

                    handle it. Also, ask your partner to reflect back to you how you seem to be feeling about the problem you have chosen.

GABI   Wow.

KASTOR   Yeah. It's the big one.

Beat.

                    Well…

GABI   I already knew he cheated on me.

Kastor stays quiet.

                    Before that night when I found him crying and said he'd cheated… Almost a year before, I'd gone through his phone. I'd found messages from numerous women on there, going back months… There were even pictures of him with them.

KASTOR   Did you tell him?

GABI   Didn't see the point.

KASTOR   Even when he admitted it to you?

GABI   It was already over.

KASTOR   Why didn't you say anything sooner?

GABI   He stayed with me. I couldn't give him what he wanted so he found it elsewhere, but he stayed with me. That must have meant something.

Transition.

KASTOR The final part of the experiment is sustained eye contact. You look into each other's eyes for four minutes.

Transition.

Kastor and Gabi look into each other's eyes. This can last anything up to four minutes but can be shorter. At the end of this time Gabi kisses Kastor. Kastor takes Gabi by the hand and leads her into the caravan. He turns the lights off and they undress each other. They climb into bed and have sex. Kastor is clearly in charge of the situation, but there is still a gentle and tender quality to the act. It is not romantic, but more than simply platonic. It is affectionate and intimate, but not heated. It is unclear if they both climax or when it happens. They both relax and lay next to each other.

Transition.

Kastor climbs out of the bed as if trying not to disturb Gabi and puts on some form of clothing to cover up. This is more due to it being cold rather than any feeling of modesty. During this speech we see Gabi dress herself and walk out of the caravan as if avoiding Kastor.

KASTOR So, that happened. It only took her, what, just over six months. Be honest, who thought we'd actually even get to this stage? (*If members of* *the audience don't raise their hands, ask why not.*) **And you know what, she actually wasn't that bad to be fair. I mean I've certainly had worse.**

When we finished we both got dressed and she left. It was the first time she ever left without saying she would book another visit. Now don't get me wrong, I know the whole point of the visits was for her to build up to having sex and enjoy it, but I was surprised how cold she became. Almost instantly. Maybe she still didn't enjoy it after all. I half expected to get a booking or something saying she wanted to meet but… I'm not bothered. Just surprised. I just got used to our evenings of chatting and what not. Actually, I tell a lie, I did get one thing. Just over a week after we had sex I got a package.

Kastor runs inside and grabs a book from under his pillow. He comes back out with it. It's a copy of 'Turn Left at Orion'.

This arrived. No note or anything but I can only think it was from Gabi. *Turn Left At Orion*. It's a guidebook for the stars and the night sky. Just a little something to say thank you I guess. Maybe she did enjoy it. I've never been given a gift before from a client. It's sweet.

A year went by. Nothing much changed. I've started getting messages from this new guy though. Haven't met him yet. Might be a time waster. He says his name's Kian, but there's something about him... He keeps messaging with these weird cuckold fantasies. I don't know. It's all money at the end of the day.

And, after I'd given up all hope I got a message through. A booking. Gabi. It took me by surprise. It was the same day and time as she always had before. And as she always had been before, she was early.

Transition.

Gabi enters wearing a pair of oversized sunglasses. She looks at her watch, looks at the caravan door, then moves to sit in her usual camping chair. Kastor pops his head around the door.

KASTOR   I knew you'd be early.

Kastor steps out of the caravan and approaches Gabi who stands up to greet him.

GABI   Couldn't go breaking the habit.

KASTOR   What are you doing here?

GABI   I wanted to see you.

KASTOR   I gathered that much.

GABI   I wanted to apologise.

KASTOR   For what?

GABI   For ending things like I did.

KASTOR   Hey, it's fine. It's not like we were together or anything. You came for sex. You got it. Why hang around?

GABI   I know, it was just a bit… We were getting close.

Silence.

Kastor doesn't know how to respond. He turns away.

KASTOR   You want a drink or anything?

GABI   I didn't mean for things to end that way. I should have contacted you.

KASTOR   I've got squashes, tea, coffee. You know, the usual.

GABI   When I went home that night I… I contacted Richard. I told him that I always knew about the other women. And that never once did he ever make me cum.

KASTOR   How did he take it?

GABI   I also said I'd been seeing someone and that I've had the best sex of my life and I've never felt more alive.

KASTOR   Wow! What did he say to that?

Beat.

GABI   New Moon tonight. New luck.

KASTOR   New love.

Beat.

KASTOR   What's with the glasses by the way?

GABI   It's just all the glare from the headlights of other cars.

KASTOR   You're not driving now though. Take them off.

Gabi hesitates for a moment. Kastor moves toward her and takes them off for her. She lets him. She has a bruise around her eye.

KASTOR   What happened?

GABI   It doesn't matter.

KASTOR   Have you been to the hospital?

GABI   No, it's fine. It looks worse than it is. I put some peas on it. Anyway, I wanted to ask, did you get the book I sent?

KASTOR   Yes.

GABI   I was gonna put a note with it to try and explain but I didn't know what to write.

KASTOR   I knew it was from you. Thank you.

GABI   I wanted to give it to you myself.

KASTOR   That would have been nice.

GABI   But I was afraid I'd already left it too long. Then once I started building it up in my head I started to have a panic attack and then I just…

KASTOR   No, of course.

Beat.

GABI   I'm sorry.

Beat.

KASTOR   Still apologising.

Beat

               Look, are you sure you're alright. It looks like you might…

GABI   It's fine!

KASTOR   I'm sorry.

GABI   Now who's apologising.

KASTOR   Have you started seeing anyone yet?

GABI   A couple of people.

KASTOR   Wow. One fuck and you're a proper little player now.

GABI   Maybe. Nothing serious, just fun. It has been fun. You helped with that.

KASTOR   It's just confidence.

GABI   That you gave me.

KASTOR   So I did succeed then that night?

GABI   Does it matter?

KASTOR   I guess not. I just hope I helped you.

GABI   You did.

KASTOR   Good.

GABI   I just had to start having feelings for you. I never thought about the fact that maybe I just never had that sort of connection with anyone before.

KASTOR   Well, I see why you didn't message then. You didn't want feelings for me. I mean if you carried on seeing me then you obviously would have just fallen madly in love with me or something.

GABI   They weren't those feelings. I liked you. I
                 liked your company. I wanted to spend time
                 with you as a friend.

Beat.

KASTOR   I'd have liked that.

Kastor moves forward to try and touch her face. Gabi pulls away.

                 He didn't do that to you, did he? Richard.

Beat.

GABI   I've thought about you a lot recently.

KASTOR   Then why won't you let me help you? Just let
                 me look at it at least.

GABI   I said I'm fine!

Beat.

KASTOR   Ok.

Beat.

                 Well, I suppose we should get on with it then.

GABI   What?

KASTOR   Well, you've booked the hour now, so I
                 assume you only came here for one thing?

GABI   What's the matter?

KASTOR	Nothing. What do you actually want to do then? Are we just talking, star gazing or do you want to fuck again?
GABI	Kastor?
KASTOR	What? You're the one who just spent the last five minutes saying how much you thought we were friends after just leaving without saying goodbye and yet you won't tell me what happened. Are we friends or are you a customer 'cause I need to know how we're doing this now.
GABI	I...
KASTOR	In fact, wait here.

Kastor goes to the toilet cistern and gets out the money. He takes out a few notes, returns the toilet back to how it was, and then goes back to Gabi.

	Here. Here's a refund for tonight. I forgot. I've got to get a load of stuff ready for the post tomorrow morning.
GABI	Kastor.
KASTOR	Sorry, I really should have blocked it out on my calendar. It's my fault. Don't worry about it.
GABI	I'll book for another time then.

KASTOR   I'm really busy at the moment. I'll have to see.

Kastor makes his way back into the caravan, leaving Gabi alone.

GABI   I'll see you soon.

Gabi waits for a moment then leaves. After a moment, Kastor comes back out, looking after her.

Transition.

Kastor approaches members of the audience.

KASTOR   **Excuse me, could you just help me for a second? Could you just turn those chairs over for me please. And would you mind just popping inside and ripping those off and flipping that over onto its side. Thank you. And would you mind just sticking some of this tape over that for me please.**

Members of the audience rearrange the set as instructed. As they do this, Kastor asks other members of the audience to touch different parts of his body, asking one to touch his face, one to touch his arms, and wherever else Kastor feels appropriate to invite people to touch. Once touched, Kastor applies purple make-up, possibly even some red liquid, until he appears beaten up.

Thank you. You can return to your seats now.

The caravan now appears wrecked as if a fight has occurred or it has been broken into.

Transition.

Kastor is sitting on the step of the caravan with pieces of furniture and broken items all around him. The bed sheets have been torn off the bed. The pillows are on the floor. The toilet cistern has been removed. He has clearly been crying. He appears broken. He gets out his mobile phone and tries to call someone. They don't answer. He starts to leave a message…

KASTOR It's me. Could you…

…but hangs up before finishing. He waits a minute then sends a text instead.

Transition.

Kastor approaches the audience, as he has done before, as if about to speak but stops. He goes inside the caravan and pulls out a bottle of whiskey which has been hidden somewhere. He drinks from the bottle.

Transition.

Kastor returns to sitting on the step of the caravan with the whiskey bottle. The sun is beginning to rise. After a short time Gabi appears.

GABI Oh Christ! What happened? Are you alright?

KASTOR I knew I didn't trust him. I knew something was weird, but I thought I'd be alright.

GABI Who? Have you called police?

Kastor shakes his head. Gabi gets out her phone and starts dialling but he stops her.

KASTOR			No. I can't do that.

GABI			At least let me phone an ambulance then? You need to be seen by a doctor.

KASTOR			Could you take me?

GABI			Of course.

Gabi tries to help Kastor up, but he resists.

KASTOR			Just give me a minute.

She looks around at the carnage before her.

			You know you didn't need to book to see me. I wanted to help you. I wanted to help you be who you wanted to be. I thought I helped. I wanted to help. And then you just stopped coming. I thought you might have messaged or something. I thought about you. About what you might have done next, whether you'd have contacted Richard or suddenly gone on a mad sex spree or something.

GABI			Kastor…

KASTOR			It's fine. Don't worry about it.

Kastor tries to get himself up off the caravan step.

GABI   We can talk about this later. Let's get you
                 looked at first.

Kastor looks up at Gabi.

                 What?

KASTOR   He's still here.

GABI   What?

KASTOR   He came at me so fast. I was just trying to
                 defend myself. I just grabbed the first thing I
                 could. I didn't even think I just hit him. It
                 wasn't hard, but...

GABI   Where is he?

Kastor gestures to another area of the caravan. Gabi goes over to look and freezes.

KASTOR   He'd been messaging for weeks but I'd never
                 met him till tonight. He started shouting and
                 screaming about his wife. I don't know if he's
                 someone's husband or something.

GABI   It's Richard.

Silence.

                 That's Richard. He must have tracked you
                 down after I told him about us.

KASTOR   What?

GABI	I didn't think. I was just trying to get back at him. Remember, I told you that I said to him that I met someone.
KASTOR	But you told him where I live?
GABI	No. No. Just that you worked from a caravan. Oh my god, I'm so sorry. I'm so sorry. What are we going to do?

Beat.

KASTOR	Phone the police.
GABI	What? No, we can't do that, there's got to be another way.

Transition.

KASTOR	**So I think this is where I showed you at the start. Just the two of us, alone in my caravan, my home.**
GABI	It's time for us to go.
KASTOR	Ok, just give me a minute.

Transition.

Gabi and Kastor are standing in the caravan. It is dawn and the sun is shining. They are looking at each other, both feel a mix of emotions; panic, excitement, nervousness, and fear. They stand in silence for a moment, just staring at each other.

GABI   Are you ready?

Kastor nods.

KASTOR   It'll be alright. This sadness won't last forever.

The lights blow and they are left in darkness once more.